MEGAWORDS

Richard Osborne is author of the international bestseller *Philosophy for Beginners* (over one million copies sold in 30 countries). He is also author of *Sociology for Beginners*, *Freud for Beginners*, *Ancient Eastern Philosophy for Beginners* and *Crime and the Media*. He is senior lecturer in philosophy, semiotics and cultural studies at Camberwell College of Art, London.

MEGAWORDS

200 terms you really need to know

Richard Osborne

SAGE Publications

London • Thousand Oaks • New Delhi

First published in 2002

First published by
Allen & Unwin
83 Alexander Street
Crows Nest NSW 2065
Australia

SAGE Publications Ltd
6 Bonhill Street
London EC2A 4PU

SAGE Publications Inc
2455 Teller Road
Thousand Oaks, California 91320

SAGE Publications India Pvt Ltd
32, M-Block Market
Greater Kailash—I
New Delhi 110 048

British Library Cataloguing in Publication Data

A catalogue record for this book is available from the British Library
ISBN 0 7619 7474 1 (hbk)
ISBN 0 7619 7444 1 (pbk)

Library of Congress catalog record available

Set in 11/13.5pt Weiss by Midland Typesetters, Maryborough Victoria
Printed by Australian Print Group, Maryborough, Victoria

10 9 8 7 6 5 4 3 2 1

Contents

This book is for Harriet Jane Osborne-Crowley

I would like to thank Helen Crowley for her critical support while undertaking this quite arduous task. Also Elizabeth Weiss and Emma Cotter at Allen & Unwin for their diligent commissioning and editing respectively. My students at Camberwell College of Art partly prompted this volume and I thank them for their interest.

Introduction

In 1976 Raymond Williams produced a remarkable book called *Keywords*, in which he carefully analysed the genesis of certain key cultural concepts that were currently in use. His deep historical sense, and understanding of the inter-connectedness of **culture** and **society**, produced a work that brilliantly illuminated the ways in which concepts took on particular inflections in different historical and theoretical eras. *Keywords* was a living dictionary of the development of concepts and of their changing use. It is partly in homage to that work that this volume is dedicated, but it is also a response to the fact that history has already left behind most of the intellectual universe that Williams occupied. Interestingly, much of the strength, and weakness, of Williams' work can now be seen to derive from his own 'Englishness', itself a term that once seemed unproblematic, but which is now resonant of **colonialism**, Eurocentrism and the somewhat uncritical acceptance of a whole way of life. The changes that the last quarter of a century has witnessed have decentred the intellectual universe as surely as they have restructured the world of work and the nature of culture.

It is in part to trace the patterns of these changes that this book considers a number of concepts that have gained recent currency in intellectual debate. Unlike *Keywords*, however, I shall only be concerned with very recent history and with considering a number of new, and sometimes difficult, concepts that have emerged during a time of very rapid change, both in the humanities and in society as a whole. It might be said that theory itself has emerged as the high ground of much current debate, and that history has been eclipsed. These recent developments in theoretical works have been so rapid, and so widespread, that not every idea or concept can be captured. Instead, I shall be looking at some of the more central—or 'mega'—words that have emerged over the last three decades. Many ideas span different disciplines, so this book will not be a glossary in the standard sense, but a map of the links between ideas and concepts in the humanities and a broad introduction to certain approaches without which students might well feel adrift in the wide world of inter-disciplinarity.

Megawords sets out to plot the historical or theoretical shifts that have transformed the intellectual debate over the last 30 years, as well as to introduce many previously obscure or unknown ideas. **Feminism**, for example, noticeably absent from *Keywords*, is the first and most obvious of these paradigmatic shifts that have rendered many historical positions untenable. Indeed, *Keywords* has an entry for family but none for feminism; a historical stance that speaks volumes of the patriarchal system to which feminism was such a powerful response. Williams came out of the traditional socialist movement formed in the 1930s and 1940s and sought to work both within a historical framework of progressive English literary criticism and in dialogue with theoretical Marxism—traditions which have been torn apart by the forces of **globalisation**, **postmodernism**, **feminism**, **post-colonialism** and the collapse of communism. It is no surprise that Williams should be so historically constrained. In fact, he always sought to place his work within a concrete historical agenda and he would have no objection to the present rewriting of the terms of the debate. As he noted, people seem to talk 'a different language' after very short historical periods and, given the rate of social change in the last twenty years, it would be surprising if there hadn't been a radical shift in the theoretical language of the humanities.

Another major shift across the humanities has been the 'linguistic turn', a phrase used to describe the rise and rise of structural linguistics, **semiotics** and, eventually, **poststruc-turalism**. This is another area not touched on in *Keywords*.

To get a feel for the conceptual language now dominant in much of the humanities, we need a framework of reference which takes account of the complex shifts in the culture and everyday life of the late capitalist societies we live in. One of the most obvious developments, for example, has been the rise of information technology and its impact on society as a whole, an impact mirrored in the adoption by theoretical language of many terms originating in computing. Similarly, the dominance of the electronic media has given rise to much of the phenom-enon we know as postmodernism.

Postmodernism is one of the most used, and seemingly least understood terms in recent thought, reflecting the deep divisions that exist within the humanities. To outsiders, it sometimes seems that intellectual work is deeply mired in incomprehensible jargon and that the humanities, in particular, have been colonised by French philosophy. The proliferation of theory sometimes appears to back up this claim, but the counter-argument may well go that a complex reality requires a complex analysis. Academic discourse, or the language of thought, moves at a different pace to that of the culture as a whole, sometimes in front of it and sometimes behind it, but there are connections, and **cultural studies** can be seen as attempting to establish those connections.

Trying to place the way that concepts are used at a particular time is a very useful exercise, since it involves trying to create a map of the culture we occupy and its shifts through time. One key term which did not warrant an entry in *Keywords*, **deconstruction**, is now a central idea in the humanities, and aptly reflects the critical and sceptical attitude which is increasingly dominant in the humanities. Where Williams engaged with the dominant ideas of traditional disciplines, many postmodernists simply dismiss all pre-viously existing thought as **grand narratives** or delusion. Even the idea of rational knowledge as such comes under attack, and we are told that only forms of micro-knowledge are possible or probable.

The early claims of **structuralism** and semiotics in the 1960s and 1970s were always that a 'revolution' in conceptualising the humanities had occurred, and that these new modes of thought would supplant previously existing ideas, producing a 'scientific' humanities or a 'science of signs'. Theory became an end in itself, particularly literary theory, which eventually seemed to take over from simply literature, and the status of theory assumed a self-justifying position. Postmodernism can be seen as the end point of these processes, where the blurring of all boundaries between cultures, disciplines and media produces a theoretical culture of seemingly endless innovation.

At the same time, deconstruction becomes a theoretical method, a political activity, a mode of being and a philosophical stance all in one, a curious state of affairs for an idea based on an old-fashioned structuralist distinction. Ideas can be fashionable just like clothes, as evidenced by the way that postmodernism, fashionable in recent years, seems to be dying out, partly under the weight of its own relativistic confusions, but also with the return of the 'real' in the form of global economic and environmental crises. It would be fair to say, however, that the present intellectual climate is rather confused and that there are multiple voices speaking about cultures and societies undergoing rapid and complex change, so any new student of the humanities is likely to be confronted by a bewildering array of interdisciplinary ideas that initially do not seem to have any great connection or coherence.

The aim of this volume is to suggest ways in which connections can be made and certain necessary concepts taken on board to provide a link-chart through the humanities and social sciences. Despite some claims to the contrary, disciplinary borders in the humanities and social sciences are breaking down all the time, and the cross-fertilisation of theories and ideas is a reality that cannot be ignored. Jean-François Lyotard, one of the key figures in postmodern thought, described his own work as 'promiscuous' and this perhaps rather neatly captures the ethos that is dominant within the humanities and social sciences today. Postmodernism is the form in which most of this promiscuity takes place, although some consider that both of these approaches are overrated and somewhat exaggerated reactions to a shift in the cultural world of the 1980s and 1990s. Post-modernism and deconstruction are largely responsible for the exuberance of a lot of the theoretical language in use at the present time, particularly in the uncharted waters of **virtual reality**, but old historical patterns continue to lurk under the surface, occasionally poking their heads above water.

In fact there is so much theoretical production in the human-ities that very few people can keep up with the ever-changing nature of the debate. To this end, I have tried to identify a number of keywords or 'megawords' without which no self-respecting student should set sail. For each one I have attempted to provide a short introduction setting out the historical back-ground of the concept, as well as discussing how the concept acquired its present meanings, and whether they will last. In doing so a further problem is encountered, however, in that the development and borrowing of concepts from different disci-plines—what has sometimes been called **nomadic theory**—leads to a situation in which there is often disagreement about the meaning of a particular idea. Plurality, it seems, is endemic to the postmodern condition.

To understand current developments we need to go back to the dominant theoretical and cultural traditions within the humanities and social sciences out of which the present state of affairs evolved. These traditions, which reach back to the ration-alism of the Enlightenment and to the European dominance of the nineteenth century, enjoyed a period of stability and seeming continuity in the affluent postwar years, in which the Cold War flourished. Increasingly, the last decade has seen a real nostalgia for the 1950s and early 1960s, a period which, with hindsight, resonates with innocence, certainty and charm.

The intellectual horizon of the time, particularly in the English-speaking worlds, was also one of apparent calm and certain consensus. English literature, as it was known back then, was still very much an Anglocentric discipline, certain of itself and committed to the study of 'great literature' and moral values, as well as being disdainful of upstart disciplines like sociology. Ideas such as relating literature to a social context, or studying popular literature for its own sake were seen as unorthodox, basically Marxist, ideas in a period when **popular culture** and media studies were no more than a dot on the horizon. The repressiveness of that culture, and its suppressing of questions of **race**, **class** and **gender**, were facts that now seem historically unquestionable. In retrospect it was the era of the sunset of European imperialism but, at the time, many clearly felt that it was the beginning of a new era of liberal certainty and western democratic dominance. The postwar world was defined largely by the Cold War, the organised anti-communism of western capitalist powers. This rapidly came to mean that all intellectual life was structured around the pro- and anti-Marxist position. Liberalism was the dominant philosophy of the West, and Marxism was seen as both its **other** and as an **ideology** that threatened the culture of the West as much as its vaunted political freedoms. The West was obsessed with the threat of communism and, particularly in America and Australia, this obsession defined politics and culture almost entirely during the 1950s. In America, McCarthyism became the clearest expression of this long-held fear that the communists were infiltrating the arts, the schools, the media, in fact, all forms of culture. The intellectual world was divided into simple black and white dichotomies and, apart from existentialism, there was little to challenge the liberal certainties of established disciplines.

Below the quiet surfaces of the 1950s, however, there were intellectual rumblings that would ignite and explode in the

1960s. Disciplines like history, English, sociology and anthropology were particularly grounded in long-standing ideas derived from the **canon** of the great thinkers, and were essentially inward looking and conservative. Part of the radicalism of the 1960s was to challenge the cosy nationalist orthodoxies of these traditional disciplines and to give birth to a more international and critical perspective.

Academic culture in the humanities in the 1950s was almost universally part of a dominant culture whose relationship to power and society was precisely that of reproducing the cultural elite; morality, **empiricism** and **humanism** were its keywords and theory was seen, at best, as an occasional necessity. The Russian invasion of Hungary in 1956 and the British invasion of Suez marked the beginning of the end of the old imperial and Cold War eras and produced a critical realignment of thinking about Soviet communism, Marxism and the certainties of establishment culture. Many thousands of intellectuals broke with communist parties around the world over Russia's brutal suppression of change within Hungarian communism, and this defining moment eventually led to the creation of the 'New Left', which was highly critical of Soviet Marxism but still operated within a Marxist critique of capitalism.

In France there were battles between the existentialists and the Marxists and, beneath the surface, the ideas of structuralism were beginning to gain credence. The long dark night of Cold-War cultural and ideological suppression was coming to an end and critical thought was about to re-emerge from the bunkers. The New Left inaugurated a search for a critical vocabulary, for a redevelopment of Marxism, embracing the nascent anti-nuclear movement and, to a certain extent, feminism. For the first time since World War II, there began a widespread questioning of many established ideas and intellectual frameworks, and it was this ethos that developed into the political and intellectual radicalism of the 1960s.

The 1960s was a decade of extraordinary change and development which completely destroyed the orthodoxies of the postwar cultures, however long their afterlife appeared to be. This decade of transformation actually spanned from 1965 to 1976 in terms of the critical ethos that we now associate with these events but, of course, 1968 was its zenith. In a moment of over-determined congruence, the nature of politics and of cultural struggle suddenly took one of those seismic shifts that are irreversible, improbable and implosive. Society, and modes of thinking about society, shifted from delusions of stability to forms of self-doubt and cultural insecurity within a remarkably short period of time.

At the start of the 1960s, most of the colonial powers still occupied territories all around the world, the Cold War clearly demarcated East and West and conservative political parties led by old men dominated European countries. The 'winds of change', a term one politician coined in reference to Africa, in fact blew all around the world in the 1960s; student riots in France, the war in Vietnam, demonstrations and love-ins in San Francisco, the civil rights movements in American and Northern Ireland, all that once was solid appeared to be melting away. **Capitalism** appeared to be in crisis and revolution was on the agenda as a real possibility.

These changes were as much cultural as political, and produced a rebirth of feminism alongside the popularisation of drugs, sex and **psychoanalysis**. Decolonisation, aided by wars against colonial powers, began to take hold, students discovered a political voice, 'youth' became rebellious and were recognised as a cultural group for the first time and the New Left developed a new form of political **radicalism** that sought alliances between workers, students and Third World revolutionary movements.

There were similar radical movements in the intellectual sphere, when traditional disciplines came under attack from students who occupied campuses and challenged the authoritarian nature of the ideas and courses that were traditionally taught. Karl Marx was rediscovered through his early works and through the work of Georg Lukacs and Emma Goldman, as well as through radical interpreters like Max Horkheimer and Theodor Adorno, who developed a critique of **bourgeois** society that drew on Sigmund Freud and Marx. The 1960s also saw the start of the expansion of higher education, a process which is ongoing even now. This led to a changed atmosphere in the humanities and social sciences, since it was no longer simply the elite who were being taught.

Student radicalism brought politics into the academy and critical thought into the social sciences, opening up the terrain of the humanities to international trends in thought and philosophy. In literary studies there emerged a 'sociology of literature' which began to question the traditional ideas of the canons of great works and the notion of the **author**. Popular literature also began to be studied and various Marxist approaches to the study of culture and ideology came into use. These approaches gave birth to what we now call 'cultural studies', a broad, interdisciplinary term much given to appropriating all kinds of diverse approaches within its remit.

Cultural studies inaugurated a revolution in the way that the humanities looked at all sorts of cultural phenomena but, in particular, it turned its gaze on popular culture, an area until now ignored by traditional disciplines, except if there were discussion of its evil influences on the masses. Most early critics of television, for example, dismissed it as a time-wasting irrelevance. In retrospect, the rise of the electronic media during the 1960s is a good example of the different cultural processes at work that led to what we now understand as **globalisation** or, simply, world culture. It was through the **mass media**, the rise of consumption and more affluent audiences, that these new groups developed into a global, rather than a local, phenomenon, giving impetus to what was sometimes called the 'youth revolution'. It's

9

important to remember, however, that at the time no-one noticed what was happening.

There was a similar movement in the humanities and social sciences, where new movements and new stars were discovered as ideas began to spread far more quickly than previously, and where there was now an audience outside of the narrow academic elite. The sexual radicalism and civil rights movements of the 1960s also produced a political critique of the dominant outlooks within academic disciplines, which were increasingly seen as narrow agendas for the reproduction of the dominant culture. It was in this fertile ground that Marxism, structuralism, feminism and psychoanalysis grew into the complicated theoretical analyses we have today for thinking about **society**, the **subject**, sexuality, social order, literature, art, the media and almost every other facet of human culture.

Raymond Williams himself is a good example of how old-fashioned literary studies had to try and come to terms with a wider world in which the electronic media and popular culture were setting the agenda and, throughout the 1970s, he engaged (albeit obliquely) with the input of continental Marxism, structuralism and linguistic theory. In his insistence on 'tradition', however, one could feel that pull towards the complacencies of history, where people and social groups knew their places, a form of nostalgia that afflicts many in a world that changes ever more rapidly.

This dialectic between change and tradition is very powerful in the humanities and social sciences, as that which is new has a particular appeal to a younger generation, and that which carries the patina of age can often seem a form of wisdom to those who have lived in a particular tradition. Ironically, Williams was very interested in the importance of 'experience' in his work on class and culture, and it was precisely the experience of change during the 1960s and 1970s that gave rise to the radical shifts in thinking and theorising that became so characteristic of the intellectual scene. While Williams was doggedly working through the ramifications of culture and communication, the humanities became a battleground for imported theory, radical structuralism and critical feminism.

During the 1970s feminism became an ever stronger force, criticising all aspects of intellectual works, from philosophy to science, as being 'gender-blind', a criticism that was deeply resisted then and still is now. In fairness to Williams we have to say that he was battling with an ancient agenda in academia in order to make television a proper point of study, while feminism was launching an insurgency that most of academia didn't even know existed, or could not even imagine existing.

We could characterise the 1970s as the era in which the humanities took an irrevocable turn towards European philosophy, structuralism and semiotics, and in which film studies suddenly became an important discipline that was used to read television and other media. Here the central issue of **realism** came to the fore, and Bertolt Brecht's criticism of realism as an ideological form was an important advance which developed into a major critique of all forms of realism in the electronic media. Semiotics, through the work of Roland Barthes in particular, began to have a major influence, and feminism began its long debate with many psychoanalytic and sociological approaches.

While this shift towards critical European philosophy was going on, another major pattern was emerging in the capitalist world, which led to the end of the postwar boom, the end of the age of innocence and of full employment. The sense of well-being and optimism that had lasted for the 30 years of the economic boom began to fade away in the 1970s and the cosy cultural framework it had produced began to disintegrate in like manner.

With the election of a new kind of radical right-winger, Margaret Thatcher, in England in 1979, the old order was over and the new age of **economic rationalism** had begun. The fact that she was a woman was more remarked upon at the time than her extreme anti-union and anti-worker message, and her support of the doctrines of monetarism and deregulation. Some people at the time thought that she was, rather like the new-fangled computer, just an aberration. In fact, her election marked the beginning of a new world order, one in which economic rationalism and free markets would sweep the world, creating immense new wealth, seemingly endless technological downsizing of jobs and a new, flexible workforce. Governments were rolled back, intervention became a sin, and welfare was increasingly reformed to allow people to stand on their own two feet, or to become part of the rapidly emerging 'underclass'.

Culture was similarly reformed, and market forces swept through the electronic media, the universities, the arts and all of the media, changes which are still impacting both on culture and the academies. The 1980s can be characterised as an era in which these forces of **neo-liberalism** became fully global, and fully realised in almost all advanced capitalist countries. The 1980s saw the birth of the tiger economies of Asia and the Far East, in direct contrast to ever-expanding unemployment and insecurity in most of the older industrial nations. Privatisation of national assets went hand in hand with retrenchment, the limiting of union power and the steady erosion of job security, as well as massive increases in multinational profitability and the rise of an international global upper class whose wealth put them outside the scope of national limits and whose ability to move their money around the world became legendary. Australia's Rupert Murdoch is a classic example. As he built up a global media empire, he left behind his Australian nationality and assumed a mid-Atlantic persona committed to a world presence in the electronic media, which now includes China and Asia as well as America and Europe.

These rapid transformations left traditional disciplines still grappling with insubstantial realities and forced a rethinking that gathered pace during the 1980s—a period characterised by the rise of postmodernism, **post-colonialism**, feminism and **post-feminism**, cultural studies, cybernetics and **cyberpunk**, deconstructionism and poststructuralism. The entire universe has been rethought through structural linguistics, poststructural linguistics and variations of theory that place language as their central focus in one form or another.

The cultural effects of these socioeconomic changes can also be seen as producing a society in which scepticism is dominant, in which all of the assumptions and ideologies upon which western culture was based have come to be criticised, to be seen as nothing more than sets of beliefs which justified a status quo that is historically irrelevant. This is the strong version of the postmodernist critique, which declares the end of history, the end of society and the global creation of a **hyperreal** reality in which the electronic media are utterly omnipotent.

There are those in the humanities who argue that this is throwing the baby out with the bath water. Criticism of traditional ideas does not necessarily lead to adopting a position of global scepticism in which all knowledge and culture are seen as untrustworthy and to be rejected in favour of a celebration of the present as **pastiche** and parody. Theoretical work in the spaces of **identity**, **difference**, the **body**, **gender** and poststructural theories of language and **subjectivity** has created an entirely new domain of academic work that takes theory as a kind of second-level signifying system, a 'meta-theory' or mythology, that is self-referential. Introducing and contextualising the concepts that are used in this kind of academic work, and suggesting their limitations, is another aim of this book. One of the central problems for the humanities and social sciences is still 'popular culture', a lower form of culture compared to 'high culture', but one which has become the dominant force in world cultures. The postmodernists hold that there is only one culture, an electronic culture of the postmodern. Since most humanities' disciplines are rooted in the values and forms of high culture, they are generally at a loss to confront the realities of popular culture. It is this reluctance to adapt that has produced the current crisis in the humanities, a crisis which in one sense can be seen as healthy in that the humanities now have to re-evaluate their own preconceptions.

This constant reworking of both the object of study, and the means of thinking that object, is responsible for the current proliferation of theory and for complicating any introduction to the humanities. This is a difficulty further compounded by the recent rapid development of the Internet and its attendant reworking of the fields of communication, education and culture. The speed of cultural change keeps accelerating, and the half-life of concepts decays almost as quickly as the cultural popularity of mega-stars, a phenomenon which suggests that we are living through a decisive **paradigm** shift, one requiring a different mode of thinking in the humanities.

Identifying key concepts, or megawords, that are important in this process of rethinking, is the central aim of this volume, together with a commitment to debunking the complexities of conceptual works and explaining the origins and functions of concepts in this changing environment.

To put it another way, we can say that the electronic has reconfigured education and that the visual has reconstituted the written in re-defining how we think of the world. Globalisation means that theory has become trans-national: what was once a keyword has become a megaword.

Aberrant decoding

An anti-structuralist term that recognises that audiences sometimes interpret messages in different ways to the ones intended.

'Encoding' is the term used to describe the way in which media practitioners construct messages so that they can be understood by the widest possible audience, almost always the aim of media professionals. 'Decoding' is the term used to describe how people read these messages.

In communication theory there is an approach which claims that messages are encoded (produced) through one set of meaning structures and are therefore necessarily decoded (received) in the same linguistic framework and with the same meaning structures. For example, if the message is encoded as 'the Queen today went to Ascot races', it should be decoded as 'the Royal Family exercised its traditional pastime of going to the races to the acclaim of the masses'. An aberrant decoding would be something along the lines of 'decadent aristocratic family indulges its ability to hoodwink the masses as to its function in society'. In other words, there are particular messages in any kind of reporting or communicating, and how they are understood (decoded) is very much a matter of the class, gender or ideological position of the viewer.

Italian linguist and philosopher Umberto Eco first drew attention to the fact of aberrant decoding, and pointed out that there are many reasons for this activity, including a total inability to understand the codes of communication that are being used. The assumption that all viewers will understand and follow the codes of communication employed by the media rests on a normative assumption that the audience is homogeneous. In an era of transmigration, **subcultures**, multicultural society and global television, it is clearly an erroneous idea to think that one is

15

addressing a straightforward audience who share communication codes. In order to think of what an aberrant decoding might be like, one might try and think of the average peasant viewer in Bhutan, the Tibetan mountain kingdom which acquired tele-vision in 1999, watching Jerry Springer interviewing transexuals who dislike women who work as roller-skating waitresses. **Mass media** texts attempt to be closed—that is, to generate only one meaning—but the context of viewing can reinterpret the message, as can the particular audience.

Abject/abjection

The non-definable sense of horror that permeates the borderlines of self.

This is an important and difficult term used specifically by the French linguist and psychoanalyst Julia Kristeva, particularly in her 1982 book *Powers of Horror: An Essay on Abjection*. A good deal of Kristeva's theoretical work is concerned with both theorising the complex subject in language, and of looking at mother/daughter relations as being seminal in constituting 'woman'.

The importance of the abject as an idea is that it relates back to a pre-Oedipal, presignifying moment, to the embryonic existence when inside/outside is unclear, and to the spaces in our culture where that dimension operates. The abject is that borderline uncertainty, the desire to expel from the body the unclean, to be a separate entity, the confusion of inside and outside; it is ambiguous, frightening and threatening to the subject's **identity**. A sense of engulfment, perhaps the power of the mother, is a cultural theme which finds expression in horror and science fiction, a fear of the monstrous that swamps the self.

The term abject itself literally means to cast out, but Kristeva is interested in thinking about the way that a psychic sense of self is maintained through creating a boundary between the **self** and the **other**, the self and those forces that would pollute it. The abject is a point of ambiguity, of unease, at which the individual feels threatened by engulfment, by impurities, by breakdown, and around which reactions and social rituals are formed. The abject is not easily defined, however; as Kristeva says, it 'has only one quality of the object—that of being opposed to the I (Kristeva, 1982: 1). It is not a clinical term, though, as Kristeva also associates the abject with the maternal body, with women's bodies, and with the way that they are perceived as threatening, as fecund and powerfully disturbing within phallo-centric forms of thought. Kristeva's writing about the abject is very broad, encompassing the social and the individual, and she describes the abject as that which 'disturbs identity, system, order'. She considers the abject across a wide range of phenomena, from indivdual acts like 'food loathing', to works of art that deal with repression, enunciation or the horror of the abject.

This mode of thinking about the fluid borders of **culture** has been taken up by film critics like Barbara Creed (see her 1993 book *The Monstrous Feminine*); and in geography by writers like David Sibley, who apply the idea to geographies of exclusion, where the creation of spatial boundaries and the exclusion of 'filth' plays a psychodynamic role in activities like 'ethnic cleansing.' In literature, particularly modernist literature, the abject is a noticeable feature of writers like Fyodor Dostoyevsky, James Joyce, Jorge Luis Borges and modern urban writers of paranoia, horror and identity.

Activism

The extreme end of politics.

Originally defined in the early twentieth century as an act of political engagement undertaken solely by the intelligentsia, the term is now more widely used to refer to a high level of political commitment and desire for action. Activists are found across all political parties and form the core of any revolutionary movement or radical protest.

Aesthetics

A theory that attempts to explain what is beautiful, and why.

Aesthetics is the branch of philosophy that seeks to deal with the idea of taste or discrimination in art and artistic judgement. We all constantly judge whether things are good, bad, ugly, boring, ridiculous or sublime; aesthetics is the study of how or why they are these things. Describing what is beautiful or worthy of praise has a long history in philosophy, going back to Plato and Aristotle, but aesthetics as a particular sub-branch of philosophy is much more recent. The term was first used in its modern sense by German critic Alexander Baumgarten (1714–62), who was interested in thinking about what made human creativity special. Aesthetics also covers questions about the nature of art, how we define what is or isn't art, what is artistic 'taste', how we define beauty and artistic experience and what the philosophical and psychological problems are that such definitions give rise to. The real search is for what can be termed 'universal' ideas of beauty: things that can be shown to be somehow intrinsically or objectively beautiful. It is here that aesthetics overlaps with **ethics**, where there is also an attempt to create universal standards. It is a strange obsession of some cultural critics to pinpoint what can be seen as always, universally, beautiful.

Many critics of this kind of 'universalistic' approach would argue that aesthetic judgements are merely the expression of a particular group's views at a particular time, and are therefore relative. When there is a dominant group in society, and that society is stable, then the dominant group's aesthetic viewpoint will tend to appear as fixed and immutable as happened, for example, with the very traditional historical painting of eighteenth and nineteenth centuries in Britain. This kind of cultural domination is what Marxist critics refer to as an 'ideological discourse', in which a class interest is represented as the universal basis of all art. Whatever agreement there was in the nineteenth century about these things has gradually declined during the twentieth century as notions of art and **popular culture** have come under critical discussion from many different theoretical viewpoints. At the end of the nineteenth century, the term 'aesthetics' was taken over by the 'art for art's sake' movement, which saw elegance and refinement as ends in themselves. Thus in Britain a slightly derogatory sense of the 'aesthetic' as indulgence remains, mainly because of its connection with Oscar Wilde and his notorious claim that 'all art is quite useless'.

The most radical critique of traditional aesthetics is clearly that of **feminism**, since the history of aesthetics is littered with ideas about femininity, beauty and women as objects of the male gaze. Like Marxist criticism, feminism wants to consider the historical and relativist basis of aesthetic judgements and their relationship to **culture** and **ideology**. The most basic question feminism poses is that of why women are marginalised in artistic production while the work of male writers and artists is elevated to the status of the universal **norm**. The marginalising of women, and of other groups, in art and culture points to the way in which the dominant group in society universalises its male-centred ideas, both consciously and unconsciously.

The apparently simple question 'What is a work of art?' provokes a great deal of debate today, when postmodernist critiques of 'high' art and movements like pop-art, punk, surrealism and postmodern artistic practice deny the aesthetic basis of accepted art, seeking to replace it with a critical aesthetic that elevates **deconstruction** over charm and beauty. From Andy Warhol to

Damien Hirst and Tracy Emin there is a constant battle over what constitutes art and an aesthetic, and the politics of aesthetics have never been more open or apparent.

Agency

The question about whether individuals act independently, or are acted upon.

The debate about agency is an important one in sociology, **feminism** and **cultural studies** since it involves the basic question of social action, moral choice and free will. The western notion of the individual and his/her ability to act independently has been a central issue since the Renaissance, when ideas of individual action began to replace the idea of social groupings. The rise of individualism as a theoretical perspective became an orthodoxy during the nineteenth and twentieth centuries, with the question of agency at its centre. Existentialism made agency a point of philosophical faith, only for a counter-reaction of anti-individualism to appear. In the 1960s the rise of **structuralism** seemed to have buried the question of agency in its arguments that language constructed the subject, only for **poststructuralism** to revive it through the back door.

Raymond Williams always referred to the debate about agency as a struggle between the two polarities of 'individual' and 'society', and much thinking in cultural studies and sociology reverberates around which should be given the greater emphasis. Broadly speaking, the debate ranges between the determinists and structuralists, who believe that the individual is unimportant, and the phenomenologists and ethnomethodologists (culturalists), who claim that individuals create their own world. Marxists and functionalists rightly argue that in fact **society** clearly shapes its members through education, socialisation and social control, but the question is, to what extent? The difficult conundrum of agency, then, concerns social, individual and cultural change: if individuals are shaped by society, how is that society can change so much—as it has done over the last 20 to 30 years—and how do individuals change?

Theories of **subjectivity**—such as psychoanalysis, structuralism and Marxism—all seem to argue that the **subject** is constructed rather than being self-activated, and is therefore unable to exercise agency in any meaningful way. If the subject is indeed constructed by language, **discourse**, **ideology** or the formations of sexuality, then it is hard to see how self-creation does take place, and thus **cultural studies**, post-colonial studies and so on have a significant problem with this idea of agency. Michael Foucault famously declared the end of man, along with the death of the author, and discusses the ways in which discourses subject the individual, the body, to 'regimes of truth' (Foucault, 1979) or forms of social control. The subject is seen as being constructed or, as Louis Althusser put it, 'hailed' or 'interpellated' (Althusser, 1978), by the discourses of language, of ideology, of the unconscious, or of whatever social structures are seen as responsible; in this view, individual agency is more or less seen as an illusion.

Recent poststructuralist work has eroded some of this more extreme **determinism** but, at the same time, talks about a fragmented identity which seems to be a possibility of multiple identities through discursive play or consumer choice. It is not really clear, however, what the determinists' position on agency is, in fact we might say that it is avoided rather than explained.

Culturalist approaches, on the other hand, advocate a strong concept of agency, of political action, of intentionality and of experience being the basis of collective political action. This kind of approach sees the working classes as being the agents of their own liberation, and sees political struggle as being a choice, not some kind of determined structural conflict. Sometimes the culturalist position does appear to valorise *any* political action and to ignore the real power of social elites and oppressive social structures, giving rise to a rather simplistic voluntarism. This overemphasis on agency does seem relevant, however, in the face of a structuralist determinism which appears to advocate theory as a replacement for social activity, and individualism as an illusion to be read like a literary text.

Postmodern theorists claim that they move beyond this sort of **binary opposition** between agency/structuration, but it often appears that they do so by abandoning the subject to its own devices in a fragmented world of pick-and-mix identity. Feminism, on the other hand, has held on to a notion of agency which has been theorised both in the politics of **difference** and sometimes in a feminist activism which claims an essential feminine as being a utopian ideal. At the same time recent structuration theory, linked to Anthony Giddens, sets out to transcend the opposition of agency and structure by explaining how they interact in society rather than being mutually exclusive; in many ways this is the real question which underpins all of these debates. The problem of agency also relates specifically to a conception of the subject, and of the role of unconscious determinations in social action.

Agenda setting

The way in which the media set public agendas of debate.

This is a term that has somewhat fallen out of use but which, in its precise definition, remains a relevant description of the role of the media. In a society where more and more information is obtained from the electronic media, where the sources of information are becoming more limited, the media play a very important agenda-setting role. This term comes from the sociology of mass communications and refers to the way in which the media decide what is, and is not, reported on, discussed, treated seriously or totally ignored. The term was first used in the 1960s and came to replace the historical notion of the media as gatekeeper, in which the media were seen as providing a filter on the world and acting on behalf of the viewers. In newspaper reporting, agenda setting could in part be ignored by the reader but the electronic media assume complete control of the news and current affairs agenda and strongly influence the sense of what is reported.

In public-sector broadcasting there were traditional notions of political objectivity, neutrality and balanced reporting, concepts which were taken over by commercial broadcasting but which have suffered in the struggle for ratings and audiences. Agenda setting influences both what topics are presented to the audience and the way in which they are presented. It is argued that because of the immediacy and regularity of television reporting, the news agenda that is created emphasises specific, violent, exciting, simple and localised events over long-term and complex issues which may be far more important. Crime is a particularly vivid example of this process: local murders receive huge and sensationalised coverage whereas complex foreign news is often relegated to the end of a news programme or ignored totally. The gratification of the audience's desire for thrilling news, and the ratings battles that deliver audiences to advertisers, means that reporting agendas are restructured by commercial imperatives. Such news agendas are an ideological framing of the cultural universe and impact directly on politics and democracy. One American professor of communications famously argued that if Abraham Lincoln were alive today, he would never be elected president because he was tall, ugly and spoke badly, characteristics which would never work on television. The television event is now a central part of the news agenda of most television news, and the manipulation of media coverage is in itself a political profession. Media agendas are set by what are termed **news values**.

Alienation

A term loosely used to describe angst, disaffection or revolt.

This is a term that has many uses, from the everyday to the legally specific, and the context in which it is used determines its meaning. Strictly speaking, the word means to separate oneself from something or to disown someone; in legal terms, to transfer the rights to something to someone else. Its evolution from this original usage to its current somewhat vague use has a long and complicated history which takes in religious use as well the philosophical use to which thinkers such as Georg Hegel, Ludwig Feuerbach, Karl Marx and the existentialists put the term.

The term is generally used today to describe living in a world from which the individual feels estranged or cut off, a condition that is seen as typical of modern society. The change in the meaning of the term began when it was used to describe a sense of living in a world over which the individual had little or no control; for example, Marx used the term to describe how the worker was 'alienated' from his labour. This interpretation has become increasingly used in the twentieth century as the individual has come to assume less and less importance in a rationalised, bureaucratic society.

The concept has fallen out of favour in the social sciences and humanities recently, mainly because of its Marxist connotations, but also because it has entered everyday language as a catch-all phrase for discontent. The idea has also become strongly associated with the postwar existentialists and their avant-garde rejection of **bourgeois** society and cultural norms. The existentialist notion of alienation came to be seen as a particular moment of angst and this was rejected by the structuralist and postmodern intellectuals.

In sociological terms the concept relates to the idea of humankind's estrangement from itself in the modern world, by which is meant the feeling that one's innate nature is distorted by the complexities of living in an ever-increasingly bureaucratic modern society. It was Jean Jacques Rousseau who first talked about (wo)man losing himself in **society** and needing to 'return to nature', and this gave voice to what was to become a constant theme of industrial society. Marx gave the concept its most thorough sociological basis and made it an integral part of his social theory. For Marx, capitalist society created a structure in which humankind's true **nature** was repressed by the economic organisation of society and in which the true essence of humanity was 'alienated' from itself. Industrial—or commodity—production meant that the worker was divorced from the products of his/her labour, and as others appropriate what is produced, this also alienates the worker from the processes themselves, from his/her own nature and from others. Alienation is therefore seen as an inescapable condition in industrial society which can only be overcome through the revolutionary transformation of society. The **essentialism** of this approach has been much criticised, since there is no 'natural' human nature to which one can appeal.

Recently there has been more emphasis on the social and psychological aspects of alienation, deriving from the existentialist sense of dislocation from society, but this use of the term is nearer the sense of **anomie** which Emile Durkheim discussed. Despite the limitations of the term, it is clear that the underlying experience of 'non-belonging' is a typical and powerful factor in present-day society.

Alterity

From 'alternative', an idea of the other, of 'otherness'. (The mother of all others.)

This term has been adopted to describe the post-colonial, post-structuralist sense of thinking about **identity** and the world in new and historically uncontaminated ways. It posits ways of thinking about the **other** that does not just place them as some kind of alien other, but as a different kind of moral being, not so much 'other' as simply different. If one begins with the simplest idea of **self**, of identity, then it is possible to think of the 'other' as being entirely outside of and different from the self. In philosophical, in feminist and post-colonial thought, the term 'alterity' is used to describe a radical other.

For René Descartes, the self was the key point of consciousness, the privileged starting point of all knowledge, and the question about the other—other forms of consciousness—was a philosophical question about how the other could be known. This kind of philosophical inquiry became a set of standard questions about knowing the other, and therefore the term alterity came into use to distinguish the newer debates about the concrete subject in post-colonial and feminist thinking.

Rethinking **subjectivity** within these new paradigms of **cultural studies**, linguistics and **feminism** has, however, presented its own problems in that the notion of radical alterity seems to imply a **binary opposition** which reproduces the older debate about self and other. In post-colonial theory, the term is used to describe the process whereby imperial culture constructs the other, the **colonial subject**, in its relationship to the self-identity of the colonising subject, which is to say that they are inextricably bound up with each other.

Androcentric

Centred on the male.

This is a historical term coined early in the twentieth century to describe the male-dominated outlook of most traditional thought. It means 'male-centred' or, more simply, 'male bias' and refers to the way in which a masculine point of view is put

forward as the **norm**, often entirely excluding women. Philosophy, for example, which claims to be the highest form of
thought, often had nothing to say about women at all, unless it
was that they were possibly beautiful, useful, feeble-minded, or
all three. The unconscious assumption that what men thought
was naturally, and obviously, more important than anything else
has been very powerful in traditional thought.

Feminist criticism of the sciences, the humanities and all forms
of uncritical thought has been one of the most powerful redefining elements of the humanities over the last 30 years. Admitting
androcentric views poses great difficulties for many academic
disciplines, however, since accepting the validity of those views
often undermines the historical fabric of a discipline's underpinnings. The gender-blindness of many approaches sometimes
seems to confirm the claim that language, too, is 'phallocentric',
that is, it is centred on the name-of-the-father. Feminist scholarship has been concerned to demonstrate the ways in which much
academic production is fundamentally, and unconsciously, androcentric, and despite the fact that these critiques are partially
accepted, it remains the case that the academic world, like the
public world, is still a male-dominated domain.

Feminism and **cultural studies** have waged a strong and
critical campaign against received ideas and ideologies, and
deconstructed the mythologies of 'objectivity' which, of course,
often turns out to be a partial and historical viewpoint. In recent
work the term phallocentric has tended to replace androcentric.

Anima/animus

The feminine and masculine principles of the unconscious mind.

Psychologist Carl Jung coined the term 'anima' to refer to the
feminine side of men. It is the **archetype** of 'woman', which for

men is embodied by one's mother. In abstract and creative terms the concept of 'muse' is another aspect of anima. Jung later introduced the analogous term 'animus' to refer to a woman's archetype of man. It is interesting to note, however, that he failed to define animus in as much detail as he did anima.

See also Archetype, Collective unconscious

Anomie

Normlessness (a product of social disintegration).

This term, which is most closely associated with the work of the French sociologist Emile Durkheim, literally means 'being without norms' or, in other words, living adrift in society without any of the rules that govern normal behaviour. Durkheim's most famous work was *Suicide* (1897), in which he considered the results of the breakdown of the social frameworks which bind people into a society or culture, and why people commit suicide. In both modern capitalist and postmodern societies, anomie becomes more and more pronounced as traditional ideas, patterns of behaviour and religions become less and less important. Sometimes used interchangeably with the term **alienation**, anomie refers to the way that life in extended communities, with clear-cut life patterns, is increasingly being transformed into isolated individual and nuclear family life in which social contact and rules are much more nebulous. The social glue that used to bind local communities, particularly rural communities, is dissolving in an ever-expanding urban life in which the individual is becoming more important than the family. The decline of community and social rules or mores generates disorder, crime and the growth of what is termed an 'underclass' points to whole sections of society who exist in a state of anomie.

Some media studies approaches consider the way in which

anomie is exploited by mass communications, particularly advertising, to give a false sense of community to those isolated and fragmented by **society**. There is also considerable debate about the effects of extensive **mass media** viewing of violence, where anomie and anti-social behaviour can be reinforced by glamorising violence. The decline of community is the subject of constant debate in sociology and **cultural studies**, while **postmodernism** implicitly claims that the electronic media have created a **hyperreal** community in which anomie is both a condition and a pleasure. **Globalisation** and global communications systems have further contributed to the decline of traditional communities and to the production of anomie. Such feelings of isolation are exploited in present-day societies by numerous fringe groups and **cults** who offer extreme solutions to these dislocations. There are some theorists who celebrate anomie as being the condition of postmodernity and welcome the possibility of anonymous and endless individual choice.

Aporia

A seemingly irresolvable logical difficulty or serious perplexity.

This is another term taken from the Greek and pressed into service by the poststructualists, particularly Jacques Derrida. In its original meaning, it referred simply to a seemingly unsolvable logical problem that was articulated by the speaker, rather in the fashion of a Greek tragedy, in which knowing your fate didn't necessarily change it. For Derrida the aporia is the nodal point of the text where all the (unconscious) contradictions come to be expressed, and it is in this fashion that it is used by the deconstructionists.

Derrida uses the term to refer to the point at which a text seems to call attention to its own inability to resolve logical difficulties, a point reached through deconstructing the text to the point where its excess of meaning is manifest. This excess of meaning, which goes beyond logic, is the philosopher's lodestone that deconstructionists find, to varying degrees, as a presence in all of the texts that they examine. There are some doubts about this approach.

Appropriation

Exploitative borrowing from a different culture.

A pejorative term used in both postcolonial theory and the arts. Artists frequently borrow from other artists and other cultures and where this is not acknowledged, this is appropriation. Appropriation is not as easy to detect as plagiarism, as it involves cultural concepts, forms and beliefs.

Postcolonial critics see appropriation as a form of cultural rape by the colonising subject. In the 1970s it was seen as a form of **activism** for white writers to write sympathetically about coloured and **black** subjects. In the 1990s however this was seen by minority writers as cultural appropriation in that their voices were being 'usurped'.

Arbitrary

The argument that there is no necessary connection between the signifier and the signified.

This is an important idea in Ferdinand de Saussure's linguistic theory, and therefore in **semiotics/semiology** generally. What Saussure argued was that it is incorrect to think that there is a natural relationship between **signs**—words, representations, **signifiers**—and the things that they represent—the object, the world, the signified. The word 'philosopher', for example, does not inherently relate to some essential nature of philosophers, but only represents the notion of philosophy through an arbitrary (or unnatural) relationship. In other words, words do not have a natural relationship to the things that they represent, but only an arbitrary, constructed one.

Having used the term 'arbitrary', Saussure then points out that the nature of the relationship is only determined by convention, meaning a cultural convention among speakers of the language. The point is that different languages have different representations for the same thing; for example, the English word 'snow' has an arbitrary relationship to the thing itself, and is very different in different languages. Saussure's discovery—which is sometimes said to be revolutionary—that this relationship between the signifier and the signified is arbitrary has had extraordinary consequences in structuralist and poststructuralist theory. All he actually seems to be saying, however, is that there is no necessary or natural link between the phonetic and the conceptual sides of the sign.

Archaeology

A mode of writing history that is non-idealist, that is, 'effective history'.

Michel Foucault uses this term to describe his rethinking of the relationship between **knowledge** and **power**, in which he attacks the generally accepted ideas of the historical importance of experts and of expert knowledge. For Foucault there is always a connection between ideas and the way in which they are deployed in **society**, and the way that this deployment exercises power. Like many of the concepts he employs, he does so in an idiosyncratic way, giving it a meaning that is highly specific to his work. His 1972 book *The Archaeology of Knowledge* sets out to unravel traditional histories of ideas which, he argues, seem to produce a coherent history of development conforming to the notion of progress. Foucault claims that there is no essential logic to history that can be shown to emerge over time but simply discourses, or discursive practices, that exhibit certain regularities. His archaeology is the illumination of these structural regularities and the codes of their organisation. Foucault claims that there are two major periods in the development of the human sciences: the classical and the modern. He argues that in these periods, which run respectively from the sixteenth to the eighteenth centuries and from the nineteenth to the present day, disciplines exhibit a particular 'well-defined regularity' which are the 'laws' of knowledge. Archaeology describes these laws.

The history of discourses is the history of their internal rules and structures, their interrelationships, and their articulation over time. The archaeology of knowledge is the way that these modes of thought are organised and produced; it is an approach to the formation of bodies of thought that looks at the way they emerge, develop and sometimes decline. Foucault's archaeology looks for the rules that govern the relationships between the terms of the **discourse**, which, he claims, cannot be reduced to academic disciplines or to the essential meaning of something called history. In one enlightening quote he says: 'The domain of things said is what is called the *archive*; the role of archaeology is to analyse that archive' (Foucault, 1972: 130).

Archaeology is the history of a discourse from within; it claims that there is no meaningful actor or inherent logic, there are only the material effects of discourse. This approach rather puzzlingly sounds as though it merely reports the development of discourse, as though no other discourse could be possible, but Foucault insists that he is only interested in the deed. The well-defined regularities that Foucault discovers do not constitute a structuralist system, he argues, but are what 'makes manifest the modes of the order of being'. To avoid the accusation that he therefore merely empirically describes historical formations, he claims that archaeology avoids this problem by considering the discontinuities of discourse as well as being aware of history being written from the present, which is, as Friedrich Nietzsche argued, the only way it can be written.

Archaeology is, then, a mode of understanding the rule formations, the emergence and development of historical discourses and their forms of existence, without either freezing them in time, or of presupposing their logic; or, in other words, without being a motiveless analysis of structural inevitability. This is a highly abstract and formalistic understanding of the structures of knowledge, one in which a structuralist **determinism** can be seen to be at work, despite Foucault's claims otherwise. Foucault himself later moves away from the rigid methodological principles he deploys here and concentrates on what he calls the genealogies of specific ideas or discourses. After 1968 he became interested more in the way that discursive practices form power relations.
See also Power.

Archetype

A powerful, universal symbol.

Symbols such as snakes and the Flood appear across all cultures. Drawing on the analysis of these common symbols contained in Frazer's *The Golden Bough* (1915), contemporary psychoanalyst Carl Jung saw archetypes as being embedded deep in humanity's **collective unconscious**. Jungian thought sees archetypes manifested in dreams, myths and works of art. The notion of archetypes has been criticised by feminists as patriarchal, since it implies unchanging, underlying gender characteristics, for example The Wise Old Man and The Earth Mother.
See also Collective unconscious

Articulation

A structured but flexible relation between parts in a cultural system.

Recent **cultural studies** have turned away both from reductive or determinist ideas about **culture** or the unified subject, and from the idea that culture can be reduced either to an expression of the economic or of a general category of structuralist analysis. The use of the term 'articulation' has now become central to modern **cultural studies** theory.

In historical Marxism, the term was used to describe how different economic modes of production coexisted within a particular epoch.

Louis Althusser also used it to describe the way in which different levels of the economy coexisted within a particular conjuncture. At its most basic level the term refers to the fact that society cannot be conceived as a unified totality but as a site of conflict and interrelation. The use of articulation derives from structural linguistics, which claims that language has a 'double articulation' in that signs consist of sounds and images, and the way they are combined together; the production of meaning is dependent on this double articulation, and that this is a model for **culture** itself.

Recent cultural studies have been centrally interested in the relations and representations of **identity**, **gender**, **ethnicity**, **subculture** and **class**, and in the way that representation can articulate the different and complicated relations between these categories, rather than reducing them to epiphenomena of economic totalities. Stuart Hall has argued that articulation can be seen as 'the theory or method of cultural studies' which refers also to the way in which different theoretical approaches can be harnessed in order to understand and analyse changing cultural identities.

Audience

The assumed group at whom mass communications are aimed.

Before the rise of mass communications, this term simply meant the group of people to whom an event, **communication** or performance was addressed, and by implication the audience were part of the process. The development of mass communications replaced this fairly close relationship with one of distance, power and impersonality, thereby changing the nature of the audience significantly. Early mass communications, however, thought of the audience simply as an agglomeration of individual viewers or receivers who were seen as fragmented and passive, but now almost everyone is part of an audience, and understanding the relationship between the communicators and the audience has become a central part of **mass media** studies.

Historically, media studies has theoretically had a 'top-down' view, looking first at the broadcasters, then considering the text or programme; often the audience was simply thought of as being an 'effect' of the process. The first major distinction that was made in terms of the audience was that between the 'audience' for public-sector broadcasting and that for commercial broadcasting. Public-sector broadcasting was seen as paternalistic, concerned with national values and civic virtues and therefore likely to seek a strong identification with the target audience (the-audience-as-public). The rise of commercial broadcasting was seen as creating a different type of audience, one concerned with entertainment, advertising and marketing (the-audience-as-market). The principles of these two different kinds of broadcasting were expressed as being, on the one hand, to serve (audience-as-public) or to sell (audience-as-market).

This rather simplistic model in media studies has been replaced by conceptions of audiences as being multifaceted, diverse and more active in their **decoding** and understanding of media cultures themselves. Both kinds of broadcasting are actively seeking audiences, and as the mass media multiply and change so the assumed audience becomes an ever more complex reality. Many recent television shows now feature the audience as central characters in the programmes, and docu-soaps are also a new manifestation of the audience becoming a self-reproducing part of the mass media.

See also Fake TV

Aura

The halo that was once thought to surround 'great' works of art.

This term was used by Walter Benjamin, a German philosopher loosely attached to the **Frankfurt School** in the 1930s and early 1940s. He used it to describe the mystical, almost mysterious, halo that was thought to surround works of art and religious objects. In his famous essay 'The work of art in the age of mechanical reproduction', Benjamin argued that techniques of mechanical reproduction such as printing and photography led to the destruction of that aura. Benjamin was ambivalent about whether this was a good or bad thing, since he sometimes seemed to be arguing that mechanical reproduction led to the destruction of tradition and the democratisation of art and literature, which presumably is a good thing.

Benjamin, however, also connects aura to involuntary memory, a complex process that he sees as being a partly unconscious state of affairs. Again Benjamin seems to argue that the mode of mechanical reproduction affects this process of involuntary memory, and thus the way that works of art are consumed and understood. Benjamin's work is notoriously complex and his notion of aura is mostly of interest to philosophy rather than to cultural and media studies.

The term is now more often used in the everyday sense that certain stars and film personalities are said to have an aura of greatness, or 'charisma', about them, which is related to the mystical sense of the word as used about religious figures and objects. The notion of the aura of an original work of art is also bound up with debates about **authenticity** and 'originality', concepts that have come in for a good deal of criticism under **postmodernism**.

Authenticity/authentic

The real or original, as opposed to the inauthentic or 'fake'.

This is an oddly complicated term that is often used in **cultural studies** and in postmodern debate but which also has a philosophical meaning that derives from Martin Heidegger. Authenticity in its most general usage is obviously a normative concept that relies on its opposite, the inauthentic. The term as used by Heidegger was taken up by the existentialists, who talked about the individual living an 'authentic' life, that is, taking responsibility for his/her life and not accepting the social situation in which they found themselves. This notion of authentic **identity** is much criticised by structuralists and poststructuralists, who see the idea as essentialist and humanist. In other words, they argue that there is no such thing as 'authentic' human nature, or even **subjectivity**, and that therefore it is ridiculous to talk about what is, or isn't, authentic. It is much the same argument as the one about **agency**: clearly, if individuals are free to act, then the question of authentic behaviour becomes important; conversely, if subjectivity itself is an illusion, then authenticity/inauthenticity is also a non-existent problem.

In talking about **culture** and cultural production, the term 'authentic' often crops up, particularly in the context of First-World theorists talking about Third-World cultures that are held to be 'authentic' as opposed to western culture, which is seen as corrupt or shallow. This line of argument goes back to the **Frankfurt School**, who argued that the 'cultural industries' of modern **society** produce superficial and mass-produced commodities that replicate false consciousness, and which are opposed to the 'authentic' and critical products of traditional high culture.

These kinds of problems are found in many intellectual approaches to the world, opposing 'false consciousness' to scientific truth, or revolutionary consciousness to **bourgeois** ideology, or women's culture as opposed to patriarchal culture. **Postmodernism** would obviously take the position that these sorts of oppositions are inherently flawed, representing a binary division of the world, and would claim that there are no pre-given meanings to texts, artefacts or cultural events. Meaning is seen as being constructed through the acts of reading, viewing, consuming or creating texts and **inter-textuality**, and so there are no 'authentic' texts, simply an endless play of textuality.

Strangely enough some postmodernist theorists, for example Jean Baudrillard, use the idea of the 'authentic' in a slightly old-fashioned way to refer to the 'real' instead of the simulacrum that now constitutes the real. In the world of art dealers and antique sellers, the notion of 'authenticity' as guaranteeing the origins of a work is terribly important in gaining the right price for an object, and it is perhaps in that context that authenticity in the modern world should be seen. The idea has an aura of psychological need related to it that plays an interesting function in the postmodern search for identities and cultural certainties.

Author/authorship

A once simple idea which has become a sociolinguistic minefield.

The idea of an author is one of those concepts that at first sight appears to be merely commonsense but which, on examination, carries a complicated baggage of assumptions. The basic idea of someone who creates a work is clear enough, but the historical meaning keeps shifting. We say, for example, that William Shakespeare was the author of the greatest plays in the English language, and this can be understood by anyone. In fact there are complex debates about whether Shakespeare even wrote the plays, or pretended to because of censorship, or for money, or whatever, and the whole question of authorship immediately becomes one of markets, **culture**, censorship, status, genius and history. The question 'What is an author?' points directly to assumptions we make in our culture about the way things work in terms of artistic production and consumption, and opens up a whole series of other questions about texts, readers and reading.

Many earlier cultures saw authorship as almost an unimportant matter, since many works were passed through oral cultures and in different versions. It is only with the Renaissance, with its ideas about mankind at the centre of the universe, and the rise of printing, that the notion of a specific author begins to be accepted. The development of the notion of individualism in post-Renaissance western societies clearly strengthened the idea of the individual author. The rise of Romanticism in the nineteenth century led to the notion of the individual genius and set the pattern for the twentieth-century celebration of the 'great author'. The nineteenth century had also seen the development of a larger reading public which was served by the professional author, and that process eventually led to the twentieth-century creation of best-sellers and **celebrity** authors.

Literary criticism studied the author to discover the roots of the text's inspiration in the life of the author, or in the character or 'genius' of the author. The author became an authority figure to whom the reader bowed down, and literary criticism mediated between the reader and the writer. These links were part of a wider set of social relationships which were characteristic of modern capitalist society. In the last three decades these assumptions have come under sustained criticism from many quarters, and the whole notion of the author has been attacked. Feminist literary criticism often pointed out that the notion of the author was implicitly male, and that the reader was also assumed to be male, thus making the concept limited at best. Marxist literary criticism tried to shift the focus away from the author towards social conditions and **ideology**, with varying degrees of success, but it was the advent of **structuralism** that led to what has become known as the 'death of the author'.

In a famous 1968 essay provocatively called 'The death of the author', Roland Barthes argued that the **cult** of the author was a glorification of individualism that gave precedence to the idea of the author as the God-like creator of the absolute meaning of a work. Barthes argued for a kind of readers' revolution in which they also were engaged in creating the meaning of a text. Barthes' argument is part of the poststructuralist attack on the idea that there is a final, fixed meaning to any work.

This movement away from traditional notions of authors and readers was continued by Michel Foucault in 'What is an author?' where he argues a strong anti-humanist, anti-individualist line, further downgrading the status of the individual author and pointing to the creation of discourses that dictate the relationships between authority figures and the implied readers. Foucault ends up talking about 'author-functions', by which he means the different ways in which an author is seen in **society**. When we talk about an author we are implicitly using an idea of a particular kind of writer who writes in a certain manner, and we react in a way that is dictated by those 'author-functions' and which reproduces the idea of the authority voice of the individual. It is important to realise that for Foucault the person who writes the work and the author are not to be seen as the same person; the author is an imaginary concept that occupies a particular place within certain relationships. There is no fixed identity giving the work its final meaning, only a series of readings which are organised by the culture we live in.

Ultimately we can say that **poststructuralism** has shifted interest away from the author to that which comes before: **intertextuality**. For Barthes and Foucault it is not the author who writes, but language that speaks; it is not the work that is the site of privileged meaning, but the text that is the place of cultural quotations echoing across the spaces of the reader.

Authority

Who's got the biggest stick?

Authority is a concept most commonly discussed in sociology and political philosophy. The nineteenth-century sociologist Max Weber defined three ideal types: legal-traditional (rules and laws), traditional and charismatic, to which more recent sociologists have added professional authority. The **state** is perceived to have authority as long as its laws and rules are accepted by the majority of its citizens. Authority is not held by the individual but rather by the symbolism of their social position, for example, a police officer. Political realists, however, perceive authority as a form of coercion. The concept is also used in the sense of 'reliability' or provenance regarding information in the humanities. Traditionally, those who belonged in the **canon** were considered to be the true 'authorities'.

Base/Superstructure

In Marxist theory the base is the economic foundation on which the rest of society—the superstructure—rests.

The notion of base and superstructure is the central idea in classical Marxism, and thereby in a great deal of nineteenth- and twentieth-century sociological thinking. The nineteenth century saw the rise of thinking about how **society** functions, with French philosopher Auguste Comte coining the term 'sociology' in the 1820s. Marx's highly original contribution to this new line of thought was to introduce the terms 'base' and 'superstructure'. In a series of works written in the 1850s and 1860s, Marx developed the theory that was to bear his name, and in which base and superstructure played a pivotal role.

For Marx the economic organisation of society was the fundamental factor that determined the overall nature of a particular society: its laws, its **culture**, its social forms and, ultimately, its ideas. This is what he meant by arguing that the economic base is the real foundation of society and that this determines the superstructure, or the secondary factors of a society's functioning. It is clear that this is a powerful argument since it is obvious that a peasant society organised in a feudal hierarchy around agricultural production is a very different kind of society to one organised around capitalist principles of profit and technological development. The model of base and superstructure points to the fundamental way in which all aspects of society are interrelated, but it does not clarify exactly how they are related.

The difficult question is to what extent, or in what way, the economic base determines the superstructure: does it totally determine every part of **culture**, law, literature, social behaviour, politics and religion, or is the relationship reciprocal, distant or even autonomous? The claim that the economic base determines everything in the superstructure is known as **determinism**, a concept that has been much attacked in **cultural studies**, **feminism** and **postmodernism**. On the other hand, the idea that the economic organisation of society influences the shape of culture and **ideology** is routinely accepted in sociology and cultural studies. Whether society can be divided into these two categories of base and superstructure is now often contested.

A good deal of cultural studies, and literary studies, has been dominated by the debates about the base/superstructure problematic and, in particular, the question of ideology. If the economic base is seen as determining the cultural superstructure, then the effects of that determination will be seen in the modes of ideological existence of cultural artefacts, which must be read in the context of this determination. Marxist literary criticism, for example, is concerned with reading the texts of literary production to understand their expression of, and relation to, forms of ideology.

Terry Eagleton has been the most prominent Marxist literary critic of the last two decades, developing a complex theoretical position that takes on board a good deal of linguistic theory but which still advocates thinking in a base/superstructural fashion. Frederic Jameson has also continued the debate in a wide and interesting manner, particularly in *Postmodernism or The Cultural Logic of Late Capitalism*.

Behaviourism

Claims to be the objective study of observable behaviour.

An empiricist approach to psychology, developed by J.B. Watson in the 1910s, drawing on Pavlov's research on animal reflexes. Behaviourism was a dominant force in American psychology until the 1960s. Behaviourists consider that data which are not verifiable by observation, for example, mental states, are not acceptable as valid scientific evidence. Behaviourist techniques have been used successfully to work therapeutically with subjects with neuroses and phobias.

Behaviourism has been critiqued as an excessively mechanistic account of human motivation and, although behaviourism has had some notable therapeutic successes, psychologists have been criticised for using behavioural techniques to treat 'deviants' such as homosexuals. Behaviourism implicitly rejects psycho-analysis.

Bias

A common-sense term that refers to the need for, or a lack of, 'balance' in the media.

This is a term that derives from public-sector broadcasting and from liberal theory in general. Its opposite is objectivity, and thus the idea of bias plays a pivotal role in liberal theories of the media. Bias is a one-sided picture of events, or of the world, and is also counterpoised to balance, the idea of an even-handed approach to news reporting. Clearly the term implies that there is both an objective world which can easily be reported and that, through balance, a fair representation of all views can be achieved. This is a deeply ideological position that, like liberalism, claims that everyone has equal access to **power** and **culture**, a position that hardly anyone involved with media studies would agree with. The idea of a truthful reporting of a natural world assumes both the existence of a universal truth and of a natural world, something that **postmodernism** in particular would strongly dispute.

Historically, the idea of value-free broadcasting was the **ideology** upon which the BBC was founded, and it is an important aspect of its defence of its privileged position. Indeed, while the BBC was the sole broadcaster in Britain it was essential that it held this position of balance. The arrival of commercial broadcasting in the 1960s and the ever-increasing domination of market forces during the 1980s and 1990s mean that this argument now has far less credibility. The news agenda of broad-casting has become more and more narrow, and more and more commercially orientated, so that the question of bias and balance is hardly raised. There is an unspoken agreement that market forces dominate in electronic broadcasting, and the competition for audiences has meant that balance is replaced by the search for ratings.

Many media critics have argued that it is not overt bias that is important in considering the ideological role that the media play in society but the unconscious bias that structures messages and agendas within a patriarchal and conformist framework.
See also Agenda Setting, Fake TV.

Binary oppositions

A fundamental division of all culture/communication and modes of thought.

The notion of binary oppositions is central to structuralist thought. It represents, it is argued, an either/or system that is found everywhere in human communication, **culture** and lan-guage. The central structuralist argument is that meaning is generated through opposition and **difference**. The argument is that humanity thinks of the world through binary oppositions, like good/evil, day/night, man/woman, culture/nature, being/non-being, and that it is the non-being of its opposite that gives meaning to a term rather than its **self/identity**. Binary opposi-tions are a product of the language system and are culturally created and sustained.

The history of philosophy is full of ideas about opposites or negations, but it is only in twentieth-century structuralist thought that the particular idea becomes so important. We can say that binarism is the very essence of **structuralism**. A lot of structuralist thought goes back to linguistics, particularly to Ferdinand de Saussure, with his emphasis on how language is structured through binary oppositions. In the hands of Claude Lévi-Strauss, this idea of binary oppositions is spread to all human culture, and he developed a structuralist mode of deciphering how it all worked. The problem is that this rather neat way of dividing everything up can be seen to be a false opposition; good and evil are rather slippery concepts once you start to analyse them, as are male and female. The eastern concepts of yin and yang rather make the point, since they are opposites but are seen as interdependent and interactive.

The belief in fixed genders—male and female—is one of the most strongly held in western thought, and is the basis on which much of culture and **society** is organised. Fixed identities play an important psychological role, however, and the threat that **feminism** poses to entrenched ideas and attitudes can be measured by the hysteria with which it is confronted.

Structuralists divide the world up into opposites and then analyse how the oppositions structure the way that meanings are created. Poststructuralists make the rather obvious points that most of the categories are not mutually exclusive, nor do things have a fixed meaning which allows such oppositions to be set up. Jacques Derrida argues that the terms in these oppositions are never equal, that there is always a hierarchy in which one term is dominant over the other. One of the aims of **deconstruction** is to unravel these hierarchies and analyse how they operate in western thought. Binary oppositions appear in much of the recent debates about difference as well.

Bisexuality

A concept that includes masculine and feminine characteristics.

Bisexuality can be seen as a troublesome term since it undermines the fundamental binary division upon which all agreed sexual identities and roles are based, being situated somewhere between heterosexuality and homosexuality. Interestingly, bisexuality has historically not been thought of as a sexual identity, but as being somehow a series of relationships, or acts, towards other sexual identities, and as such it has not been stigmatised in the way that homosexuality has been. This tells us something about how **identity** and **difference** operate within systems of meaning, and also about how masculine and feminine, heterosexual and homosexual categories work in oppositions.

In biological terms bisexuality refers to the presence of male and female sexual characteristics in an organism, and this sense of duality permeates its use in cultural terms. Sigmund Freud used the term to refer to the existence of masculine and feminine psychological characteristics in the human psyche, and pointed out that originally all individuals are effectively bisexual, or polymorphously perverse. It is also interesting that historically bisexuality has rarely been a topic in literature and art, except in the dramatic tradition of cross-dressing. A notable exception is Virginia Woolf's work, especialy her novel *Orlando* (1928) and her non-fiction *A Room of One's Own* (1929).

Bisexuality troubles everyone, including gays and lesbians, despite the fact that it clearly challenges normal heterosexuality. Bisexuals have sometimes been labelled 'temporary homosexuals' or, even more disparagingly, 'weekenders'. Some theorists have argued that seeing bisexuality as existing 'between' two opposed forms of sexuality only serves to reinforce that polarity.

Black/Black politics

A difficult and politically loaded term that is the site of much debate.

The politics of colour encompasses one of the most vibrant cultural struggles of the last 20 years, and the issues it raises are critical to our understanding of cultural politics. In colonial history 'black' has always been an identity of subjugation, of oppression, and reclaiming a positive identity marks the transition from black to black politics. There cannot be more politically loaded terms than 'black' and its associations, from the negative of 'negro' to the positive of 'black is beautiful'. Black consciousness, black politics, black studies: these are all terms that cluster around the consciousness of **race**, and of the reality of racism.

Franz Fanon, the great Algerian theorist of colonial oppression and the politics of racism, wrote an important paper he simply called the ' The Fact of Blackness' in which he drew attention to the way in which the perceived **difference** of colour made discrimination that much easier. Black studies developed a cross-cultural perspective on the history of oppression and slavery that constituted the history of the African **diaspora**, and developed a critical black consciousness. **Cultural studies** also drew attention to the way in which populist discourses drew on common-sense 'biological' notions of race, which formed the basis of official racism about supposedly inferior races. The historical connections between western imperialism and 'whiteness' meant that racism was an institutionalised part of the very operation of **colonialism**, and that 'black' was always constructed as the historical **other** and as the object of oppressive policies. The history of thinking about race and racism has been a long and difficult one, and it is only since the political and cultural struggles of the 1960s that it has been a central question in cultural studies. In fact, it is probably only in the last decade that the question has moved from the periphery to the centre of cultural studies. For a long time cultural studies was undoubtedly ethnocentric and allowed race to be invisible, thus black studies had to put the question of difference onto the agenda and question the unconscious assumptions on which such ethnocentrism was based. The questions of **identity** and difference that are so prominent in cultural studies today point to the centrality of settled ideas of **ethnicity** and 'whiteness' which underpins much of an uncritical discussion of **culture**. Furthermore, the question of race and 'blackness' poses the question of **multiculturalism**, of cultural dominance and of a reworked cultural order that is increasingly on the agenda.

Black studies is both a part of, and a major critique of, cultural studies; it is also an integral part of what is now called postcolonial studies, centred on the black diaspora, what Paul Gilroy has called the Black Atlantic diaspora. Black studies developed mainly in the United States but has had influence around the world since the questions of race, identity and ethnicity have increasingly come to the fore in the postmodern world. Confronting the cultural roots of racism undermines the liberal and universalising pretensions of cultural studies and also calls into question the forms of theoretical study within academic disciplines, which are themselves often colour-blind. Replacing ideas of race with notions of ethnicity has moved the debate forward, since biological notions of race have been comprehensively debunked as racist ideology, but the problem of colour and racism within liberal multicultural societies is still an unspoken agenda.

One of the most complicated areas in black cultural studies is the relationship between black music and fashion and its white counterparts; black music is hugely influential, hugely profitable and exists in an uneasy symbiotic relationship with the music and fashion industries. As exemplified by rap music, black can be a signifier of cool or, as in the case of Michael Jordan, a global signifier of success, but this coexists with a cultural system in which racism is still institutionally endemic. It is possible to argue that the idea of black has itself become commodified within sport, fashion and music, and that such incorporation is itself a feature of postmodern society. The question then returns to one of identity and identity politics.

Body

The bodily mechanism, the site of discourses about the body.

The fact that the concept of the body has become one of the megawords of recent theoretical debate strongly suggests that in the last two decades there has been a major historical shift in thinking about the personal and the physical. This shift in the discourse about the body has been brought about by the influences of **feminism**, Michel Foucault and **queer theory**. These kinds of theories set out to challenge the common-sense idea of the body as a natural, biological entity.

From philosophy's beginnings, the dominant intellectual tradition has conceived of the body as something external to the mind, or as a problem or a kind of prison from which the spirit escapes. At the same time the whole conception of the body tended to be uncritical; it is another term that seems to have led an innocent life for a very long time, emerging in rationalist thought as the opposite of mind, but always seen as an unproblematic, natural reality. In these traditions the body was thought of as a physical entity, as a functioning system that was analysed by anatomists and medical practitioners, sculptors and artists, but not by sociologists or philosophers.

Historically, Sigmund Freud and psychoanalysis changed this approach dramatically, producing an idea of the imaginary body, and the ego, or forms of self-identity, as very problematic ideas. The power of the unconscious and the idea of biological drives made the relationship between mind and body, idea and physicality, material and ideal, much more complicated, and thus perceiving the body as a simple mechanism was no longer possible.

The rise of **feminism** in the postwar era also led to much more questioning of both the idea of the female body and the nature of **gender** and sexuality. The female body, particularly, became the site of theoretical debate within feminism, with Simone de Beauvoir seeing woman as being a prisoner of her body. Other feminist approaches distinguished between sex as biologically given, and gender as socially constructed, but the female body was still seen as a problem.

More recent views of the body see it as a concept that is deeply implicated in naturalised and ideological views of the world. In other words, the body is no longer to be seen as a simple material reality, but as a complexly constructed object of social discourses. The biological body, whose essential character has always been assumed to be male or female, is now, particularly after Foucault, thought of much more as being the product of discursive regimes. The body is in no sense a natural or simply physical reality, nor is it a particular sexuality or sexed body; instead it is seen as an indeterminate potentiality. The problem in understanding the body in contemporary cultural discourse becomes one of developing a theory of the body while still recognising that it is experienced as a material, physical presence.

Understanding the body has become something of a preoccupation in recent cultural and feminist studies because of changing political realities, post-feminism, and the many questions that arise about health, **race**, **identity** and **power** within a society in which the body is also becoming commodified. Like **subjectivity**, the body is the real, the immediate, the experienced, and in a sense one has to stand outside it to understand it, which makes theoretical thinking difficult. Sometimes the term 'embodiment' is used to describe the way in which the bodily bases of individuals' actions and interactions are socially structured: that is, embodiment is a social as well as natural process.

We can no longer accept the argument put by second-wave feminism that women are the **reality** of their biology, that the female body is the site of authentic identity. The body, male or female, is increasingly seen as being altered and shaped by the social pressures of fashion, political fashion, body fetishism, consumerism, health awareness, body-building and plastic surgery. The body is the final frontier and many are travelling there to reconstitute it in the image of their choosing. It can be argued that, as a result of developments in genetic engineering, reproductive technology, body-building techniques and plastic surgery, the body is less and less a given fact and more and more just a possibility, an option. The implanting of technical devices in the body to keep it functioning, and the regularity of transplants, means that the boundaries between bodies and technology become ever more blurred. The **cyborg** body is clearly not far away and this kind of development threatens common-sense ideas of the body on which much of everyday discourse is founded.

In post-colonial theory, much attention is paid to the way in which stereotypes of the racialised body have operated to maintain discourses of oppression, and to bolster biological notions of race. Franz Fanon drew attention to this question and, more recently, Foucault has extended this discussion of how the body becomes the subject of regimes and 'embodiments' of particular power structures. Increasingly it is being recognised that the body, then, is a much more complicated reality than common-sense approaches would have it. The lived experience of the body is continually developing and changing, and cultural theory has to move with it.

Bourgeois

Originally a Marxist term describing the propertied classes.

Marxist theory defines the bourgeoisie as the middle classes whose wealth depends on the labour of others.

With increasing industrialisation, 'bourgeois' became a term of abuse meaning elitist, reactionary, anti-working class and pro-establishment. This sense of bourgeois persisted into the twentieth century and broadened during the 1960s to include a

notion of morality based on convention and respectability. It is a portmanteau term of abuse which was taken up by youth sub-cultures and avant garde artists as symbolising all that was outdated in **society**.
See also Capitalism, Class.

Brand

The commercial name of a particular commodity or series of commodities; their composite image.

From Nike® to Coca-Cola®, brand names dominate **consumption** and **culture** in the capitalist world, and in most of the global culture. Creating and maintaining a brand name has become a major socioeconomic strategy in global capitalist culture. There is an intimate connection between branding (creating and maintaining a brand name) and advertising, which reinforce each other as image industries in defining the parameters of consumer culture. It is clear that the branding of merchandise represents another step in the commodification of culture, and in the blurring of the distinction between consumption, culture and socioeconomic being.

Brands are signifiers as well as being marketing realities, and they play a very important role in postmodern culture. A brand name gives a consumer object an extra dimension, a mysterious life of its own which is beyond the object and yet part of it. Coca-Cola® is the most well known brand in the world and its brand name is estimated to be worth US$54 billion, of which a large part is the intangible value of the name itself. Interbrand, a consultancy that specialises in researching and analysing brand names worldwide, produces an annual survey of brand-name activity which ranks the world's top one hundred brand names by value. Coca-Cola®, for example, is shown to have tangible assets, buildings, production lines, equipment and stock that is equivalent to only one-third of its market value or, in other words, some US$30 billion of its value is comprised of its brand name, its image.

Sociologically speaking, this phenomenon is both vital to understanding global culture and relatively under-theorised. Jean Baudrillard in part addresses the question of consumer culture and its ideologies when he argues that new consumer mythologies are the way in which 'our entire society communicates and speaks of and to itself'. For Baudrillard, however, the entire social world is swallowed up in a frenzy of communication and hyperreality in which the specificities of the existence of brands simply become another moment in the ambience of postmodernism. Brand names are the way in which consumption is now organised, and the way in which global culture communicates with its mass audiences, and understanding them requires a sociology of brand names that unpicks their development from advertising slogans to cultural artefacts. In fashion, for example, brand names are very significant, codifying certain aspects of cool and of being fashionable, a system of meaning that constructs consumption as an endlessly repetitive process. Branding is also a form of recognition within mass electronic culture, a means of group identification that extends across all aspects of consumption, from novels, music, musicals, cars, films, clothes through to TV programs. Brand names are effectively the grammar of global consumption, and have to be considered in this light. Various **cultural studies** approaches have looked at this from a semiotic point of view but have mostly ignored the socioeconomic organisation of the branding process, which increasingly structures production and consumption.

The electronic and symbolic economies of the global marketplace depend on the policing of brandnames for their proper functioning, and the production of 'fake' brand-name goods highlights the symbolic importance of the image in economic terms. Microsoft®, the world's second largest brand name after

Coca-Cola®, is currently under investigation by the American authorities for anti-competitive behaviour, in other words enforcing its control of global software through improper means.

Such a case highlights the fact that brand names underpin huge multinational conglomerates whose turnover and power is often greater than many national governments. This aspect of **globalisation** is increasingly important in cultural studies but has not received a great deal of attention. The centrality of advertising in the creation and sustaining of brand names, and the encroachment of advertising into film and television narrative—the inter-textuality of branding and entertainment—are also important aspects of this reorganisation of culture.

Bricoleur/Bricolage

A complicated idea about the creation and definition of cultural heritage.

This is a term unique to Claude Lévi-Strauss—who operates with an anthropological definition of **culture**, rather than traditional cultural analysis—in his analysis of myth and contemporary society. It is important because it emphasises the way in which he sets out to construct the relationship between modern and primitive thought through analysing myth. The term fits into his structuralist re-reading of all culture as signsystems, but is also a term that has been picked up by later structuralists and poststructuralists. In his important 1966 work *The Savage Mind* he refers to the way that mythical thought is created out of whatever materials are available: 'whatever is at hand'. His argument relates to the way that particular cultures function with their own specific ideas and content—the bits and pieces that make a material discourse—which are constructed into a system of signs with characteristic structures and rules. Lévi-Strauss claims that the sign systems of primitive cultures are more motivated than those of so-called 'developed' cultures, that the connection between the **signifier** and the signified is more functional, more effective. The reference point is always the way that cultures operate like a language, with a grammar that is unseen to the primitive mind. This leads Lévi-Strauss to argue that this helps us understand modern cultures more effectively as we see the way that modern, and postmodern, cultures create the diverse and abstract sign systems within which we operate.

A bricoleur is the name given in France to a sort of odd-job man, someone who makes basic repairs using any available materials; bricolage is thereby the result of his activities, a sort of patchwork of elements. For Lévi-Strauss, the structuralist understanding of the way in which underlying patterns emerge in cultures that have seemingly different content is his major intellectual breakthrough. Other theorists have drawn on this recognition that culture does operate as a kind of intellectual bricolage rather than as a defined and historically orderly process.

Roland Barthes took this kind of thinking into the modern era with his *Mythologies* (1959), which was a structuralist reading of the peculiarities of popular culture. In considering seemingly random things like wrestling, food, flags and flowers, Barthes looks at the way that culture 'as a system' operates. In much postmodern thought there is also a recognition that many elements of culture are objects that are found and reconstituted into new patterns; indeed, this plundering of both other cultures and the past is characteristic of postmodern culture.

Jacques Derrida also argues that most intellectual work is, in fact, like bricolage, that the necessity of borrowing one's concepts from wherever they may be found in the philosophical heritage, in the ruins and reconstructions of all texts, is today a given. From literary texts to art installations, from music to **cyberpunk**, the reconstitutive patterns of bricolage are everywhere on show. The term is also used rather interchangeably with 'collage' or 'montage' in the arts and film.

Bureaucracy

The layer of officials who invent procedures to control societies.

Generally this term is used in a hostile sense to refer to officials, procedures and systems of power that have come to dominate 'advanced' societies. Franz Kafka's novels often evoke the seeming irrationality and abstract power of these systems, and in this he pointed to a fundamental feature of modern life: 'the iron hand of rationalisation'. In its more sociological sense the term refers to a specific system of administration, a set of rules and regulations by which an organisation attempts to fulfil its goals.

German sociologist Max Weber gave the term a clear description and argued that it was a central concept in the development of modern societies. He claimed that bureaucracies had a 'rational' character, based on rules, specialisation, hierarchy and a strict **division of labour**. Impersonality and the impartial application of rules were meant to ensure that a bureaucracy operated efficiently, rationally and fairly. This ideal type of bureaucracy supposedly bred efficiency, and in some periods this may have been the case. Kafka's prescient sense of the irrationality of bureaucracy is the antidote to this rational optimism, and has been born out by the monstrous bureaucracies of Nazism and Stalinism.

In the last two decades the New Right have made a political creed out of attacking bureaucracy and 'red tape', and promoting anti-government government. This in itself demonstrates how much the problems of bureaucracy and rationalisation have penetrated our very complex societies in which multinational entities, rather than governments, appear to control much of the socioeconomic world.

The split that bureaucracy creates between the public world of rationality and the supposed private world of family and emotion reflects both historical divisions between masculinity and femininity and between work and leisure. Postmodern society appears to be breaking down many of these categories but bureaucracies are seemingly highly resistant to change, and computerisation adds to the dominance of systems over responsiveness to aims and goals. The sociology of organisations, looking at how bureaucracies grow even within the smallest organisations, is an important area of recent research.

Camp

Originally an affectionate term for an exaggeratedly effeminate style in homosexual men, it is often used more broadly to refer to **queer** culture.

Canon

A list of approved texts, orginally of a religious character.

This concept is derived from religious use in which a canonical text is one that is divine, or has the imprint of authority. In literary and **cultural studies** this is translated into the idea of a canon of accepted great works. In literary criticism this idea of the accepted great works became ever more important as literary studies developed within national cultures. Indeed, a good part of literary criticism became a discussion of which works should, or should not, be allowed into the canon. F.R. Leavis, the radical English literary critic, was famous for redefining the English canon as being only some of the work of just four or five writers, but his interpretation of the canon has been much criticised.

There is obviously a connection between the construction of a canon, the teaching of literature and the creation of national cultures. In Britain this has always been centred around William Shakespeare and other great (male) writers who are held to reflect the qualities of what being 'British' means. The nineteenth-century era of British imperialism saw a particular redrafting of the canon to include writers who, like Rudyard Kipling, reflected this imperialistic ethos, and it was in part against this that Leavis reacted. His humanistic redrawing of the canon created the basis for a more enlightened sense of literature but it, too, reflected a narrow agenda that has been characterised as 'dead white males', particularly by feminist literary criticism.

Since the 1960s, the accepted canon of literary works has come under fire from many quarters, including women, black and working-class writers, and from ethnic groups once marginalised by the white European canons that held sway in academia. This decentring of literary discourses has provoked much debate and some, like Harold Bloom in *The Western Canon* (1994), have made attempts to reassert the universality and validity of western literature.

Clearly the creation of a canon of works, whether by an individual author or a series of authors, is a process of institutionalising literature, of creating an accepted hierarchy, and this process must always be one of reflection and change, something which is not always accepted in traditional institutions. Studying literature alongside other texts, within the structures of cultural production and consumption, seems a more rational approach than attempting to de-historicise and reify particular texts.

Capitalism

An economy or society organised around commodity production for profit.

This concept describes an economic system that came into being in the sixteenth century and which developed to become entirely dominant in Europe by the nineteenth century and globally by the late twentieth century. The term was first used in the nineteenth century by economists, but Karl Marx and other socialist writers made capitalism, as a system, the enemy, whereas conservatives often claim that capitalism is the highest form of democracy. Capitalism is characterised by the commodity form of production, in which labour, technology, science and, ultimately, **knowledge** are brought within these forms of economic organisation. At the core of the capitalist mode of production is the exploitation of labour-power, where the worker is separated from the means of production and their labour-power transformed into a commodity. Labour-power is the lifeblood of capitalist society, and exploitation is the central nervous system; profitability is the religion and class conflict is the product.

Within capitalism, eventually everything is transformed into commodities, including art, literature, sex and, in postmodern society, relationships. The idea of capitalism as a total socio-economic system derives mainly from Marx's sociological writings, and thus it has always had a negative connotation. It is true to say, however, that Marx also emphasised the revolutionary technological dynamism of the capitalist form of organisation, which has proved to be more correct than his analysis of inevitable crisis. However, Marx's emphasis on technology and the means of production as key factors in capitalism's development has proven to be an important insight.

Capitalism is seen as having developed from primitive commodity production (which existed alongside feudalism) through mercantile capitalism (in which profit came from trade and conquest) to industrial capitalism (the revolutionary phase of technological development) and into monopoly capitalism (where larger and larger conglomerations control capital and production). The post-communist era has seen the emergence of a global capitalism in which the market is paramount and in which commodity production, and capitalist commodity markets, seem dominant. The present form of 'late capitalism' is sometimes characterised as postindustrial society or, more recently, as the information society, in which the forms of commodity production and consumption are conceived as having developed to an almost post-capitalist level where they are globally dominant and irreversible. The cyber-economy and the ever growing dominance of the Internet and e-trade suggest that capitalism is indeed moving into a new era. The unanswered question in much of the social sciences, media studies and humanities is simply whether these areas of **cultural reproduction** have now been commodified too, and what the role of capitalist social relations in the sphere of knowledge production means for the role of theory in **society**.

The question of the relationship between capitalism, **race**, **class** and **gender** relations has been much debated, with hardline Marxists attributing all social problems simply to the dominance of capitalist social relations. Marx and Friedrich Engels argued that women's oppression derived from the requirements of **bourgeois** society and the origins of the family, which provided servicing to the labour force. It was argued by socialist feminists that domestic labour was part of a non-waged labour force that reproduced the capitalist system in the family. Later feminists criticised these approaches as being economically reductionist, since patriarchy had existed before capitalism and was not the same thing. **Culture**, language and **ideology** have been examined for their role in reproducing patriarchy, and their relationship to capitalism as a system has become a central issue in much recent **cultural studies**.
See also Base/Superstructure.

Carnival

An idea of how subversive forms of popular culture can be, and their history.

The importance of this term lies in its unusual and critical stance in understanding how **popular culture** can function in relation to dominant power structures, a critical position which both underpins some postmodernist ideas about **culture** and subjects them to a critical political viewpoint. The term comes out of the work of Mikhail Bakhtin, in particular his 1984 study of François Rabelais in which he considers the importance of the carnival in mediaeval and Renaissance society, and looks at the way that 'carnival' functions as a mode of popular **counterculture**.

Although his analysis is of particular historical epochs, there is a deep resonance within his work both with the suppression of popular culture under Stalinist regimes and with the anti-state forms of carnival that now exist within advanced capitalist countries. That is to say, Bakhtin prefigures Antonio Gramsci's ideas about cultural struggle and the way in which genuine radical working-class culture threatens and usurps the decorum of dominant cultures. In forms of carnival, Bakhtin argues, there is a truly folk culture in which the distinction between participants and viewers is broken down, and in which individualism is replaced by anarchic communal disorder. In this boundless, oppositional culture there are the germs of real resistance to the power and pomposity of hierarchical society, and this spirit of community and mockery has given rise to the political tradition of cultural resistance that is still alive.

Bakhtin argues that the symbolism of carnival is most clearly represented in the crowning and subsequent de-crowning of the king/queen of the carnival, a mockery of the powerful symbolism of the sovereign and a powerful political rehearsal for real events. Bakhtin claimed that the traces of this radical dissent and comic satire of elites was passed down through mainstream culture via the work of Rabelais, William Shakespeare and Fyodor Dostoyevsky, among others.

Bakhtin's argument that traces of the carnivalesque were found in modern culture was taken up by John Fiske who, in his work on postmodern cultures, claims to find carnivalesque elements at work in present popular culture. In particular Fiske argues that a strong anti-elitism is found in popular culture and also that the elements of the grotesque are also emphasised in popular entertainments such as wrestling, body-building, boxing and the freak shows of daytime television. Fiske also argues that profanity and vulgarity are clear elements in popular culture, similar again to the suspension of everyday limits on profanity in carnival.

Interesting though this argument is, it seems a very long historical journey from the feudal world of drunkenness, violence, death and blasphemy to the polished and safe world of daytime television, however irreverent the presenters might appear to be. Carnival was public, uncontrollable, based in the mass activities of crowds and expressive of a primitive and violent culture; postmodern culture, on the other hand, is controlled, electronic, individualised and based on a highly sophisticated marketing system that plans out viewers' reactions. They are about as similar as a fancy dress party and catching the black plague, the latter being far more common in mediaeval times than organised leisure.

Castration complex

A psychological fear of castration, this is a key idea in the Freudian theory of sexuality.

This idea can only be understood within the framework of Sigmund Freud's analysis of the development of human sexuality and of the acquisition of **gender** as a form of socialisation. For Freud this complex centres on three main experiences: the fantasy of castration; fear of the father; and the puzzlement of children over the discovery of anatomical differences between them, in particular, the presence or absence of a penis. The idea of a castration complex is a central part of Freud's theory of how individuals come to develop 'normal' sexuality and male and female gender roles.

Freud's ideas about how subjects acquire a sexual identity in society have ramifications across all the social sciences and humanities. The castration complex occurs, Freud argues, when the little boy both desires the mother and realises that the father is a threat to him, may symbolically castrate him. According to Freud, the boy's possession of a penis and the girl's lack of one lead to different forms of the castration complex. The boy fears castration whilst the girl assumes she has already been castrated; both, however, defer to the father, to the law of the father, and thus enter the Oedipal phase. The boy becomes heir to patriarchal law while the girl must accept her complete inferiority, leading to penis envy, or neurosis, or to love of the father. The question in the humanities is to understand the way in which these developmental stages are represented in character formation, ideals about individuals and expressions of the relationships between the genders. Many feminists have challenged these ideas, particularly that of penis envy, as being phallocentric, whilst some have rejected Freud altogether.

The work of French psychoanalyst Jacques Lacan transformed Freudian approaches and also offered a reworked notion of the castration complex, which some feminist writers have taken up. In Lacan's version of the castration complex, it is language, not biology, that is at the centre of the transformation. His basic argument is that both boys and girls are seen as being castrated, but the biological question of the penis is only a symbolic reality; it is the subject's position in relation to language that is important, the **alienation** of the self who is not in possession of language. The representation of the phallus in language (what Lacan calls the symbolic order) places boys and girls in differing positions in relation to **power**: for women it is about lack, and for men it is about loss. Thus the castration complex works through language but asymmetrically, conferring on the male a privileged position. In both Freud and Lacan, then, understanding masculinity and femininity as social construct requires an understanding of the deep psychological structures of the castration complex.

See also Phallocentrism, Power, Psychoanalysis.

Celebrity/Celebrity culture

A famous person, someone who is globally known, a star, and the culture that creates this phenomenon.

The term 'celebrity' hardly qualifies as a concept; rather, it is a postmodern portmanteau word that carries a great deal of cultural weight as the signifier of how electronic and media culture operate. The term has been used since the 1920s but has only gained its current status since the 1960s, and its particular global resonance in the last decade.

Stars like Madonna, David Beckham and Britney Spears only exist in electronic culture, and are part of the secularised religion that is the basic underpinning of celebrity culture. A celebrity takes on the character of a mini-god in much the way that, in the Hindu religion, there are many gods, major and minor, who intermarry, feud and interact with mortals. Thus there are a race of celebrities to answer every kind of need in the search for identification and audience participation; there are sporting celebrities, film celebrities, music gods, models, actors, television announcers and now celebrity chefs and writers. To be a celebrity is to occupy a different universe to that of ordinary people; it is to be glamorous, rich, exciting and larger than life.

It is interesting that the term, as originally used, applied to 'showbiz' and referred specifically to a particular group of Hollywood stars who were carefully controlled by the large studios; the term has now spread to all parts of the media and to many different individuals, with complicated consequences. Where Hollywood stars of the postwar era could act out their public life while maintaining a private life, the present-day celebrity is part of a constant media scrutiny in which the celebrity 'lives' the celebrity life in public. This transformation of human relationships through the electronic media has many peculiar consequences, one of which is that many fans feel that they know the celebrity intimately, and that they share ideas and tastes. That this kind of identification through the electronic media is a common feature of postmodern culture is demonstrated by the efforts that celebrities have to go to in order to avoid their fans, the most persistent of whom are labelled celebrity stalkers.

The electronic media cultivate intimacy with the individual viewer/listener, and yet this intimacy is entirely false and constructed at a distance, a distortion which produces behaviour in many viewers which can only be described as psychotic, however mild the delusions they might hold. The celebrity is, then, an electronic illusion as well as a physical individual, and this peculiar existence explains the schizoid behaviour of the media, the fans and the celebrities themselves. The truth of the other universe of celebrities was demonstrated in the infamous trial of O.J. Simpson, in which the parallel universes of stardom and the legal system imploded and gave birth to a live celebrity trial in which even the judge played to the cameras, and in which justice was the victim. Celebrity politicians are also a product of the virtual world of electronic culture, and thus analyses of the mode of being of celebrities is increasingly important in **cultural studies**.

The way in which the idea of celebrities—or 'stars', as he calls them—supports the dominant ideology of individualism has been analysed by Richard Dyer (Dyer, 1986). He points out that the elevation of the individual reinforces the idea that the 'private' sphere is of greater importance than the 'public', and that we are more our individual selves in the private sphere. Celebrities are overamplified individuals and this contradictory reality often impinges on the public sphere, particularly in the form of endless interest in the private life of stars, itself a contradiction in terms.

We can argue that celebrities replace individualism with superhuman signifiers of religious recognition, a process which distorts social relations in the interests of electronic culture. The celebrity stalker may well turn out to be the archetypal figure of the millennial imagination, a sort of image-terrorist in search of meaningful recognition. Celebrity culture is a global network of commodification, deification and dehumanisation. Its archetypal text is *The King of Comedy*, a film that presaged a whole era of celebrity-obsessed borderline psychotics.

Chaos theory

The strange and seemingly unrelated interconnections of events.

This is a theory that comes out of mathematics. It has crossed into both **cultural studies** and everyday **culture** despite the fact that it is highly complex in mathematical terms. It is concerned with the study of seemingly random activities, like the weather, that on closer inspection have an element of regularity that can be described mathematically. Chaos theory becomes important because, in our highly complex and interconnected world, trying to predict the outcome of seemingly random events would be a major step forward.

Like an urban myth, chaos theory has been propagated along the lines of 'if a butterfly in Latin America flutters its wings, this could set off a chain of circumstances that could lead to World War III'—a sort of postmodern anti-causality for **popular culture**. Chaos theory has been taken up by postmodern thinkers as a kind of metaphor for social order, but this is simply description elevated to the status of theory, or possibly the endless play of possibility.

Perhaps the right way to put the question about chaos theory is to ask why a mathematical theory, based in fractal geometry, has become a metaphor both for social order and for the study of culture itself. Or, in terms of literature and art, why have the humanities failed to produce proper models of analysis so that a mathematical model is now being utilised to explain cultural behaviour? The very idea of chaos theory itself is seen by some as a **metaphor**, since the regularities it finds in irregularities can be said to be a product of the theory itself, a 'self-similarity' produced by endless computer-generated patterning. Whether chaos theory finds the edge of order and chaos, as has been argued, is also an interesting question, but it would be fair to say that the jury is still out.

Chora

A difficult term, dating back to Plato, which has come to symbolise the underlying energy behind a system of language.

This philosophical term, dating back to Plato, has been utilised in different ways by the feminist thinkers Luce Irigaray and Julia Kristeva. As used by Kristeva in her complex 1974 analysis of language, **semiotics** and **subjectivity**—*Revolution in Poetic Language*—the term takes on a particular meaning within her overall theoretical approach, which, although undoubtedly difficult, is constantly interesting and provocative. The Greek word *chora* meant an enclosed space, a womb, and Plato defines it in *The Timaeus* as 'an invisible and formless being which receives all things and in some mysterious way partakes of the intelligible, and is most incomprehensible'.

Kristeva takes over this complicated use of the concept and redefines it to say that the chora is neither a sign nor a position, neither a model nor a copy, but prior to **articulation** and figuration and analogous to vocal or kinetic rhythm. The chora appears to be the place where pre-verbal energies and movements are contained in a kind of pre-linguistic rhythmic pattern which itself exerts pressure on the orderliness of symbolic language. The chora, therefore, contains all the heterogeneous disruptive energy that undermines language as a system, the irrationality and fluidity of pre-linguistic being which cannot be contained by traditional semiotic theory.

The term is Freudian in that it is concerned with the flow of energy in the body, and its psychic manifestations, but it is also a linguistic term in that it is concerned with the operation of language in the speaking subject. The term reaffirms Kristeva's concern with the heterogeneous and contradictory nature of language as used by the speaking subject, contrasted with the formulaic notion of language employed by traditional semiotics.

Citizenship

The idea that the individual has rights and responsibilities which must be recognised by the state.

Citizenship is rather like **nationhood**; it is an assumed reality that, on reflection, is very difficult to define. In modern democracies citizenship is taken for granted, but involves constantly changing notions of rights and responsibilities. To be a citizen is to be a member of a nation-based **state**, to have certain rights in law and often to be seen as equal before the law. The idea of citizenship owes a good deal to **Enlightenment** thought and to the ideals of the French and American revolutions, but these ideals are being undermined by the global economy and by multinational economic power.

The sociological theorist T.H. Marshall describes citizenship as being the development of certain individual liberties and rights over the last 300 years; many of these rights were the product of political struggles, like the right to vote. The fact that women in most democratic countries only obtained the right to vote in the last 100 years, and often after intense struggle, shows that the notion of citizenship was always only a partial **ideology**. The liberal ideal of the equal citizen before the law was always considered by Marxism to be an ideological description which hid the real inequalities of **power** and control, and in which political control was maintained through consensual politics.

In the modern period we can distinguish between formal citizenship, membership of a nation-state, and substantive citizenship, that is, the possession of civil, political and social rights. In the postwar era, and particularly since the 1960s, formal citizenship has become a more complicated question as immigration, dual citizenship and the **globalisation** of work forces have made the basic allegiances of citizenship rather blurred. Citizenship is also a political concept which suggests duties as well as rights; in this context the rise of a pan-European ideal and the collapse of communism have meant a further rewriting of the basic idea. Universal ideas of rights are seriously undermined by the realities of globalisation, by shifts in economic power and by the rewriting of the social contract that was held to exist between governments and citizens. The exclusion of what has come to be called the 'under-class' in modern societies is a sharp reminder of these realities to the universalising discourses of current neo-liberal thinking, and those exclusions are also seen in terms of race and ethnicity.

Citizenship is meant to embody the principles of liberal democracy and of pluralist society, and there is therefore a substantive and complex debate about how these things can be rewritten, and realised, in a postmodern global society.
See also Nationhood.

City

An urban metropolis, the centre of modernity and a place of fragmented identity.

The development of the city in the last two centuries mirrors the rise of modernity, the increased use of technology, the fragmentation and rationalisation of social living and the rise of individualism. Questions about how cities function and their impact on city dwellers remain important in cultural and post-modern theories.

The role of the city in globalised society also produces much discussion. Questions about **subjectivity** and **identity** are central here. The city is conceptualised as the space, the socio-economic community, within which place, community and **culture** are constructed and in which identity is lived out and formed. Mapping the city as place, symbol and idea has become an important strand of thinking within **postmodernism**.

Civil society

Everything in society that is not government

Civil society is the social sphere in which individuals and organisations coexist. It includes the family, private organisations and corporations. Civil society is not independent of the **state**, but rather is merged with it to such an extent it's difficult to tell where one stops and the other begins. This relationship has been called 'mutually reinforcing'. Some modern commentators see civil society as providing an alternative to the prescriptive power of state and government.

Civilisation

An Enlightenment term that came to epitomise the benefits of scientific and industrial progress.

This is another term with a very complicated history that overlaps with that of **culture** but has the particular sense of 'civilising' or of pointing to the development of organised, complex social life. **Enlightenment** rationalism saw civilisation as being a universalising process that, through scientific knowledge and reason, would eventually lift everyone out of ignorance and superstition. Civilisation was counterposed to barbarism and religious intolerance, and was instead associated with the modernising project of industrialism; it was underpinned by an optimism that has been increasingly questioned in the twentieth century. Modern civilisation has come under intense scrutiny in sociological debates which have highlighted many of the darker sides of civilisation, such as **anomie**, bureacratisation, community breakdown, mental stress and cultural and emotional deprivation. Much of the reaction of the ecological movement can be seen as a critique of the limits of civilisation, and as advocating a return to more natural, human-scale activities. Since Sigmund Freud's seminal *Civilization and its Discontents* was published, we have also been aware of the repressed side of human nature in civilised societies and of the conflict in the notion of civil order and reproduction.

Class

A social group that shares a common outlook or place in a social stratification.

The debate about class is a central one in most **cultural studies** as well as in history, sociology and media studies, but the use of the term has declined recently, partly as a result of feminist critiques of class and of postmodern rejection of the idea altogether. Class is undoubtedly the fundamental division in social stratification, by which is meant that class analysis based in the work of Karl Marx defines the basic way we think of the groups into which capitalist society is organised.

For Marx class was fundamentally an economic category, which is to say that a group's relationship to the means of production, to economic **power** and control, was the basis on which class identity was based. Many popular songs recite 'there's the rich and the poor', and this pretty much sums up the basic paradigm of what Marx was talking about. What he said was that in particular modes of production, like **capitalism**, there were social relations that conformed to the mode of economic production and distribution. In capitalism there emerges a capitalist class, whose members own and control the means of production, land, capital, factories, mines, technology, etc., and at the other end of the economic scale there are the members of the proletariat, who own nothing and who are thereby forced to sell their labour-power to the capitalist class.

This is the crude theoretical model and there are many complicating factors, like the existence of the old aristocracies, of the Church, of professional middle-class groups, of the lower class of shopkeepers and small independent artisans, but the basic divide is between the bourgeoisie and the proletariat. Marx in fact argued that all other classes would tend to melt away and that a final confrontation between the two historical heavyweights was inevitable, but this proved to be inaccurate. On the other hand, Marx did often talk about the complexity of class relations, of how different factions of the same class could have different interests, and of the way in which a class could be aware, or unaware, of its real class interests. When Marx talked about **ideology** and **culture**, he also made it clear that he understood the very complex ways in which class interest could be perceived and acted upon, so that his overall position on the way class worked in **society** was not at all simple in the final analysis.

The key difficulty in class analysis was rendered by Marx as the question of **agency** and he posed it as the difference between class *in* itself (class structure) and class *for* itself (agency and consciousness). This distinction remains problematic. Max Weber refined the notion of class to encompass skill and education, but he was still in basic agreement with the Marxist model. Weber discussed five classes: the propertied, the intellectual, the administrative, the petty bourgeoisie and the working. Weber was dealing with an increasingly complex class model at the end of the nineteenth century and he was also more aware of the complex role of the state and the bureaucracy in mediating class antagonism. Recent feminist theory has had a complex relation to the idea of class, many thinkers incorporating it into debates about structured inequality but criticising it for its gender blindness. Feminists also wanted to discuss the inequalities produced in reproduction, not just in production, and to consider how women service men and children and are thereby doubly exploited in class terms. In much class analysis women are often treated as appendages of men, and are thus unproblematically assigned the same status as men, a position that is changing rapidly as gender and social relations are being transformed. Some feminists have conceived of women as a sexual class in their own right.

Perversely, the idea of class has fallen out of favour in recent theoretical analysis, at the same time as media research and advertising agencies, as well as government statisticians, have ever more finely honed their analysis of the class composition of the population and the audiences of mass communication. In what is loosely called postmodern, or sometimes postindustrial, society one of the features of the transformation of society and industry has been the rapid decline of unskilled labour and the creation of a new under-class who have no stake in society. The fundamental relationship to the means of production is once more the most important definer of life expectancy and economic success, albeit in negative terms.

The question of the perception of class, or class imagery, is rather different in that here the debate has clearly shifted over the last 20 years. The way that people perceive the class structure, and their position in it, is radically affected by electronic culture and the culture of consumption, which repositions people as classless consumers rather than as class members. Such imagery has long been deployed as a rhetoric of the 'classless society', particularly in America and Australia, while in Britain the continued existence of class is almost celebrated as a national heritage.

Postmodernism reflects the surface debate of media culture as though it were the reality, which partly explains why postmodernists see class as being unimportant. Against this one might point out that on all economic indicators, the gap between the rich and poor over the last 20 years is still increasing. The most recent analysis of the global economy suggests that we are also seeing the rise of a new 'super-middle-class' and of a multinational 'over-class' who live globally and owe allegiance to no particular state or country.

Code

A system of signs governed by cultural rules.

The idea of a code comes from the influence of **semiotics** in literary and **cultural studies** and refers to a widely accepted set of rules or patterns that are treated as defining a particular area. There are many uses of the term, from behavioural codes, dress codes, game codes to signifying codes. The Highway Code is a good example of the potentiality of codes in that it is both a behavioural code, describing how to act when on a highway, and a signifying code, referring to knowledges about social interaction. The idea of a secret code also rather neatly explains how a signifying code can work, since only those 'in the know' understand the secret code and, in the same way, only those who understand the conventions of a code interpret it in the right way.

Literary codes, which are rather like genres in that people recognise them as particular forms (such as westerns), are good examples of how signifying codes can work. Literariness itself can be a major code, calling attention to itself to declare that this text is 'literary' rather than descriptive or educational. A code alerts the reader to the modes of signification that are being utilised, and ensures that the agreed interpretations are produced. Thus with satire, for example, if the code is not read properly, the text can be read as descriptive and completely misunderstood.

Roland Barthes, in his more structuralist moment, proposed that there was a set of literary codes by which readers could recognise elements in a work and relate them to particular functions. These codes, as Barthes argued in *S/Z*, were:

- The proairetic code: a sort of master code that controls the way the plot is read.
- The hermeneutic code: the code that explains or unravels the problems that are produced by the plot (for example, why does X murder Y?).
- The semic code: the code that contains various textual elements that advance the reader's understanding of the characters (presupposing that there are characters).
- The symbolic code: this develops the reader's understanding of potential symbolic meanings.
- The referential code: this constructs references to various cultural phenomena.

These didactic codes, rather like a mechanical exposition of how a story works, have very rarely been used by any literary critics, not even by Barthes himself, quite possibly because literature works through constantly reworking codes of meaning rather than constructing narrative as though it were intellectual Lego. Codes are always susceptible to change, being governed by conventional use, and unless structuralists can adequately define the difference between a code as a written set of rules and a code as an unspoken set of rules, then the term is not of as much use as first suggested.

Non-verbal communication is conducted through presentational codes, gestures, clothes, expressions, tone of voice, etc., although these systems of meaning can also easily be misunderstood. Barthes, however, also talks about metalinguistic codes, symbolic codes, narrative codes, cultural codes and scientific codes, among others, which merely reinforces the point that a code is just a local arrangement of particular cultural conventions to reflect common usage. As Umberto Eco points out, there is a good possibility of **aberrant decoding**, where a reader or consumer reads the code in an aberrant or opposite manner to the one intended.

Collective unconscious

Past human experience which is integral to the psyche.

A concept central to Jungian psychology which refers to the ancient, shared experience of the human race. The argument is that our day to day ego consciousness is only the tip of the iceberg. In the same way that humans share physical characteristics, they also share common dreams, fantasies, visions and **symbols**. In 1919 Jung coined the term **archetype** to refer to the specific manifestations of the collective unconscious. It is not a widely accepted idea.
See also Archetype.

Colonial subject

The subject created in colonial societies, and how imperialism shaped such subjectivities.

Thinking about the colonial subject is a key area in post-colonial studies and derives from the theoretical work of Franz Fanon, particularly his 1952 work *Black Skin, White Masks*, in which he outlined the complex psychological effects that **colonialism** induced in colonised subjects. Clearly the **identity** of an oppressed people, dominated by the language and **culture** of an invader, is going to be distorted by that process of domination, and the internalised sense of inferiority that the coloniser seeks to inflict on the colonial subject is at the centre of this discussion.

The debates around the nature of the colonial subject revolve around both the impact of colonisation and the relationship between the colonialist and the colonised. Theorists Like Homi K. Bhabha argue that there is, in effect, a dual **subjectivity** of the two, interconnected in a hybrid process. These are recent historical debates that demonstrate a huge shift in **cultural studies**, one in which the certainties of western thought are themselves opened up by the act of theorising the colonial subject and its relationship to its past.

Colonialism

The creation of colonies, and the economic and cultural domination that results.

The historical process of dominant states, cities or cultures developing colonies—that is, taking over or dominating peripheral or satellite areas—has been going on since the beginning of recorded history. What the term refers to in recent debates is the European phenomenon of imperialist domination of other countries. This phase really began in the sixteenth century with the Spanish and Portuguese domination of South America, although these two countries were to decline into peripheral status themselves in the nineteenth century when colonialism was at its height.

Colonialism refers to the way in which imperialistic countries such as Britain, France and Germany set out to colonise—that is, to occupy and transform—the countries or territories they invaded, controlled or acquired. Edward Said, the Palestinian/American theorist, distinguished between imperialism and colonialism by pointing out that imperialism was best used to describe the attitudes, practices and theory of the ruling metropolitan centre, and colonialism to describe the process of settlement and attempted incorporation that went on in the dominated territory.

Colonialism went hand in hand with the expansion of capitalist forms of society, and many theorists argue that the need for raw materials, and sometimes markets, led to the rigid dominance of colonised countries and the exploitation of the local population. An ideology of **difference**, a rigid separation, was essential to the justification of this process, and the ideology of **race** played a central role in defining and rationalising colonialism. From our historical standpoint, it seems difficult to conceive of how the exploitation and plundering of colonised countries was not only rationalised but seen as a 'civilising' mission that was in the interests of the colonised. Imperialist ideas, hand in hand with racial notions of difference and superiority, and backed up by forms of social Darwinism that talked about the survival of the fittest, justified invasion, occupation, appropriation of land, apartheid and the slave trade.

In the twentieth century much of the world has been convulsed by struggles over colonised nations, World War I being a redrawing of empires and spheres of influence and World War II the outcome of unfinished business from the first war. Much of postwar history has been dominated by anti-colonial struggles, by decolonisation and the legacy of hundreds of years of colonial domination. Throughout most of Africa, Asia and South America, the struggle to throw off colonial or imperial powers has defined most world history in the last 50 years. It is worth noting that hardly any country ever obtained full independence from a colonial power without armed struggle of some kind, a reality which somewhat undermines the claims of ex-colonial powers to have gracefully withdrawn when the time was right.

The debate now is about what form post-colonial societies take, whether they are free, or whether the world system of neo-colonialism, the global economy and Third-World debt still exercises domination over the 'decolonised' countries.

Communication

An integral aspect of all human culture; language is a central mode.

The term 'communication' originally referred to the physical systems of interaction between communities, e.g., boats, trains, postal services, rather than the actual messages carried. Gunther Kress argues that this notion of communication as a 'thing' has been replaced by communication practices, processes and mediums. So, 'communication' now can refer to almost anything, from a wave of the hand to the system of interconnected computers that makes up the Internet.

The emergence of communication as such an umbrella term means that it is a fundamental concern of disciplines across the humanities and social sciences.

To give just one example, in **semiotics** communication is a process by which messages are produced and understood in a cultural context. Semioticians consider that the methods by which a message is transferred are just as important as its content or the expected response.

Conflict theory

The idea that society is based on repression rather than consensus.

A sociological term which refers to theories developed in the 1950s and 1960s, based on Karl Marx's claim that all societies are fractured by social conflict.

Social conflict is caused by inequalities between groups, for example, **class**, **gender** and **race**, and involves disputes over resources and property, rather than **ideology**. Thus society is conceived as a site of constant conflict, and the state as the arbiter of final resort.

Connotation/Denotation

The way in which words, signs and images convey different kinds of meaning.

This is a basic distinction used in structuralist and semiotic analysis to distinguish between the literal meanings of things (raven = raven = a bird) and the potential metaphoric, allusive, second-level meanings that an **image** can generate (raven = death). Denotation is seen as the level at which a **sign** or image refers directly to the thing it names, and connotation describes how such signs or images produce secondary meanings. In film and media studies this is a very useful tool for analysing how visual images work in narrative structure, and how such images can construct a pattern of connotation through association and unconscious motivation. Whether connotations can be fixed or defined by the location and structure of a work is a more difficult question, particularly in relation to cultural artefacts that are seen across cultures and different groups of interpretive communities.

Denotation can be a fairly precise process in which a meaning changes hardly at all over very long periods. On the other hand, connotation can be an elusive, socially constructed process in which a shared cultural group can endow an object or idea with a particular, localised meaning or association. Recent semiotic work has looked at the ways in which subgroups may borrow, reinterpret or even reverse the connotations of clothes, fashions, cultural objects and forms of language. Visual cultures operate on the borders of this denotative/connotative distinction and thus it is there that determining meaning becomes most problematic. As cultural diversity increases assumed and shared meanings are harder to define and the possibility of aberrant readings grows.

Conspiracy theory

The (paranoid) idea that secret groups of people control the world.

It is a remarkable phenomenon of human psychological life that the idea of a small, secret group of people somehow contriving to dominate the world reappears with alarming regularity.

This is not to say that in certain circumstances there have not been small, select groups that have dominated certain societies or movements. Rather, the historical strength of the idea suggests that we are in the presence of a myth or paranoid structure that is deep in the human psyche. The power of this paranoid mythology is evident in the activities of the Nazis, who used the notion that secret groups of Jews were running the country and the banking systems to launch an all-out 'cleansing' of Germany and much of Europe by trying to exterminate the Jews. Many right-wing and nationalistic groups adopt this same kind of conspiracy theory, which strongly suggests that its origins lie in the insecure psychological identity of the individuals, which they then project onto a hostile world. American right-wing militia groups, Christian fundamentalists and left-wing revolutionaries all share a conspiratorial theory that tightly knit, secret groups somehow manipulate the world against them, and must be opposed and destroyed.

Many of these groups often claim that the **mass media** are dominated by a conspiracy to misreport the truth of what they have to say, and that therefore some secret group is controlling things. It is interesting that there is a very successful genre of popular literature and film—such as the James Bond films—which often suggests there are secret conspiracies that must be dealt with. That these sorts of conspiracy theories have proliferated this century suggests that they may well be connected to growing feelings of **anomie**, **alienation** and powerlessness in societies that are increasingly bureaucratic and impersonal. Paranoia is seen by some theorists as being the dominant ethos of our present electronic society, in which surveillance and control are powerful forces.
See also Anomie, Alienation.

Consumption

The act of consuming, particularly of commodities, of shopping or purchasing goods and services.

This is a concept that has a slightly peculiar history in that its use in Marxism, which is where it originates from within sociology, is derogatory, but it has developed into a whole area of debate within **cultural studies** and **feminism**. For Marx, production was the important part of the economic equation and consumption was simply the ideological end of capitalism or, in other words, exploitation. The historical transformation of the notion of consumption from that of bourgeois enslavement to a theory of lifestyle and patterns of behaviour in part mirrors the historical change from economies of scarcity, where poverty was the problem, to economies of surplus, where consumption itself can be a problem. Postmodern society places consumption as one of its central activities, whether of goods, services or ideas, and recent sociology and **gender** studies have developed a theory of the 'culture of consumption'.

Feminist approaches started from the point of view that traditional Marxist analysis did not incorporate the questions of domestic labour, reproduction and cultural relations into its mainly production-based analysis and, therefore, to understand women's different relationship to society it was necessary to think more about consumption. Consumption has been thought of in gender terms, and more particularly female terms, but that too is changing as consumption becomes ever more a generalised activity. The study of consumption throws light on social changes, on the changing nature of shopping and retail spaces, and on how leisure and consumption are becoming integrated and displaying new cultural patterns.

Roland Barthes began the turn towards thinking about **popular culture** and consumption and his work led into the poststructuralist and postmodern theories that consumption can be seen as pleasure and play. Fashion, food, cars, romance, shopping and all forms of advertising, music and the media have been considered in this new wave of consumption analysis, sometimes rather uncritically.

Postmodernist arguments talk about the ways in which **identity** can be constructed through consumption in a play of images, meaning and cultural consumption, but it is not clear where this freedom stems from or how it realigns social structures. Madonna is seemingly exhaustively quoted in this context as a purely postmodern pop-star who constantly reinvents herself. The politics of pleasure and consumption are accorded a positive role in identity creation which is seen as liberatory. This seems to underestimate somewhat the extent to which consumption is a functional part of capitalist production and distribution, and the degree to which consumption has its own price, both individually and collectively.

Copernican revolution

The metaphoric moment when it was realised that the earth moved around the sun, and not vice versa.

The so-called Copernican revolution of the fifteenth century destroyed the belief that the earth was the centre of the universe. An obvious problem with this idea as a revolution is that it took a very long time for the ideas of Copernicus to permeate the general culture, somewhat the opposite of a revolution. Similarly, the theoretical events that have been compared to the Copernican revolution are perhaps exaggerated when being described as momentous events that shocked the world.

It is, for example, often claimed that Swiss linguist Ferdinand de Saussure decentred language and destroyed the 'metaphysics of presence' that had dominated western philosophy since the beginning of time. The revolution was such that his work was almost entirely ignored for 50 years before being brought to light by the structuralists of the 1950s and 1960s. It is an interesting fact of recent intellectual history that there are constant claims that all **knowledge** that precedes the paradigmatic shift of the postmodern period is seen to be tainted and inadequate, whether it be from the 'metaphysics of presence' or the allusion of **subjectivity** as the author. The **metaphor** of revolution, and of the Copernican revolution, must be the single most overused term in the entire history of western thought.

Counterculture

A new anti-establishment form of culture.

This term was coined to describe the new wave of largely middle-class protest movements, for example, the hippies, who were protesting against the cultural values of the establishment. Although the hippies' main target was originally the Vietnam War, the counterculture also railed against the values and goals of **capitalism**, the work ethic, the patriarchy and society's dependence on technology. An anti-capitalist message was central to the counterculture.

As it is used now the term refers to any minority group opposing a dominant culture as long as it is doing so in an articulate manner. It is similar to **subculture**, but the latter is largely a working-class phenomenon. The current anti-world trade demonstrations are the continuation of this counterculture.

See also Subculture.

Critical theory

Interdisciplinary approach to social and cultural analysis.

Critical theorists use social science research methods as a force for political and social engagement. Developed first by Max Horkheimer and adopted by the Frankfurt School of intellectuals in post-World War II Europe, critical theory rapidly spread throughout Europe and America and became the intellectual basis of the New Left. Students and radicals in the 1960s and 1970s found in critical theory the catalyst they had been seeking to turn Marxist theory into effective social and political action. Critical theory is characterised by its emancipatory and reflective approach and, since the 1980s, has found its way into textual analysis in the work of structuralists and postmodernists such as Michel Foucault and Jacques Derrida. Jürgen Habermas is today's most notable critical theorist.

Cult

Small esoteric group often founded on religious belief or shared ideas.

It is interesting to note just how often this term is used in cultural analysis and **popular culture** today, in expressions ranging from cult movies right through to the sinister and dangerous activities of religious cults that are indicative of deeply anomic social groups hostile to society. The popular cultural use of the term denotes little more than an enthusiasm for a particular popular film or pop-group, what might have been called a film buff or a fan in an earlier period. A cult following suggests a new kind of fan, however, someone who is committed to the esoteric minutiae of a film or a pop group or even a football team.

At this level of obsessive interest we can see where the problems of **identity** overlap with dominant cultural structures. In a fragmented world, identifying with a specific group solves many of the problems of **anomie**. This problem of identification was touched on by Sigmund Freud in his theories of how group identification works in society, and how groups can be a way for individuals to lose themselves by dissolving into the group. Cults provide an organised form of social behaviour which absolves the individual of decision making, a process that the Frankfurt School identified in their analysis of what they called the 'authoritarian personality'. This kind of personality wants to find an external authority, like the father, to direct it in an alien-ated world, and therefore easily falls prey to charismatic leadership and social control. The Frankfurt School were partic-ularly talking about the rise of fascism in Germany and the way in which the Fuhrer, the 'Father', led a movement in which total obedience was required.

Western liberalism elevates the individual as the locus of rationality and reason, but in reality the individual, and the individual ego, are under threat in present-day culture, and the group provides a form of security against an alien world. Ident- ification is an important and complex process in **culture** and the decline of the family leads individuals to find identity in cults and group patterns. Cults from Scientology to the Aum group develop anomie to extreme lengths, and elevate the eccentric law of the father to a quasi-religious status. The weakness of the ego in modern society and the dominance of electronic media that are predicated on creating viewer identification with the presenter produce electronic cults organised around soap-operas and cult programs.

Psychological manipulation is one of the key organisational principles of postmodern consumer society, and it is therefore no surprise that groups which reject **society** form cults that mirror that kind of psychological manipulation, as L. Ron Hubbard made apparent when he invented Scientology and its methods of indoc- trination and incorporation. More recently, in America, however, it has been right-wing fundamentalist and white-supremacist cults that have been the real danger, and they have been responsible for hundreds of deaths. It is interesting to note that the cult of 'whiteness' is difficult to combat because it articulates dominant ideologies that are normally hidden and suppressed.

Cultural capital

The transmission of privileges from one generation to the next.

This is an important term that was developed by the French sociologist Pierre Bourdieu, and he uses it in a way that draws on the notion of capital itself, or economic power. Just as capital is central to the reproduction of the class system at the eco- nomic level, so cultural capital is important in reproducing social and cultural relations. Cultural capital operates in a similar way to economic power in that access to the dominant **power** system dictates how successful individuals are within the educational system, how much cultural capital they control. The term is used to refer to cultural knowledge, behaviour, taste and acceptable opinions and consumption—in other words, a pattern of social distinction and cultural consumption that fits in with the dominant culture.

Ruling-class culture is reproduced in complicated and subtle ways, and learning the appropriate patterns of behaviour is a lifelong process. In Britain this transmission of cultural capital can be seen quite clearly in the system of (private) public schools and the Oxford–Cambridge axis, in which family and history still play a very important role. While great play is made of the democratisation of cultural life in the advanced capitalist countries, there is much evidence that cultural capital is still an important mechanism in delimiting access to symbolic capital. The legal system in Britain is a historically moulded concretisation of cultural capital in which judges are secretly elected as being of the 'right stuff'; not surprisingly, 95 per cent of all top judges are from the upper middle classes and went to the top schools. The number of working-class students going to the elite universities has fallen over the last 20 years, and private schools and colleges have expanded. Bourdieu also makes the point that the idea of cultural capital is equally applicable in the communist societies of the East, where the elite can make sure that their children enjoy the benefits of their privilege and patronage, despite a lack of private property.

Bourdieu's argument that cultural domination is exercised through cultural capital is similar to Antonio Gramsci's theory of **hegemony**, which concerns the way the dominant classes exercise their cultural power through consensus rather than coercion. In cultural terms this can be seen in the way that repressed cultures often copy and replicate the modes and mores of the dominant culture. The classic teddy boys of the 1950s affected a style of dress that was directly copied from the upper-class Edwardian dandies, just as much of today's fashion apes the style and mores of the rich and famous.

Family and education are still the main transmitters of cultural capital, of accumulated cultural knowledge or behaviour, and while the media claim a democratic culture, there are clear patterns of audience differentiation which reproduce ideologies of distinction.

Cultural populism

An approach to popular culture that celebrates its diversity and anti-establishment politics.

In **cultural studies** in the last decade there has arisen an approach to **popular culture** that sees it not as the degraded mass culture of earlier analysis, but as an affirmative experience which is inherently critical and political. This cultural populism overlaps with postmodern approaches that celebrate the radical and carnivalesque nature of all popular culture.

The work of John Fiske, Paul Willis and John Docker has been highly influential in this area. In essence their approach highlights the creative and critical elements of popular culture and downplays the commercialised and standardised parts of it. What Fiske argues is that while popular texts appear to reinforce the status quo, to reproduce dominant cultural ideas, in fact many people respond creatively to the works of popular culture that they encounter, often reworking the meanings of these texts.

Fiske introduces interesting arguments about the way in which people encounter the texts of popular culture, by which we mean television programmes, films, videos, magazines, newspaper articles, etc. In an original approach, Fiske argues that rather than just absorbing the ideological messages they carry, people react to the texts of popular culture initially by evading the ideological message, then by creating offensive forms of reaction to that message. This can certainly be seen at football matches, where fans compete to recreate dominant messages in abusive forms of group chanting. Fiske then goes on to argue that acts of evasion are followed by a process of oppositional **decoding** that he calls productivity. In this phase, Fiske appears to be arguing, the meanings of the text are reconstituted at either the literal or imaginative level so as to be rendered wholly different. Drawing on Bakhtin's arguments about the nature of the carnivalesque, Fiske claims that popular texts display a kind of primitive anti-elitism, a comic disrobing of the pretensions of the elite, which is equivalent to the evasion and rejection he analyses.

This kind of metaphoric theory is interesting in the way it draws parallels across different historical eras, but it is also reductionist when it fails to differentiate between early medieval society and the mass consumer society we live in today. As a result of this kind of theoretical blurring of real situations in favour of sweeping generalisations about **culture**, Fiske is able to argue that the populist rhetoric of much popular culture is the same thing as political resistance. The problem with this argument is that it allows Ronald Reagan's populist rhetoric—a version of extreme right-wing individualism concocted out of westerns and *Reader's Digest* philosophy—to be identified as 'evasive' and 'productive'. There are power relations in all cultural production and **consumption**, and dismissing these in favour of analysing merely the surface of cultural artefacts seems theoretically innocent, to put it at its most favourable.

There are those who argue that cultural populism is the theoretical partner of free-market ideologies which argue that whatever people want, they should have, and that it is elitist to criticise the people's cultural choice. This position simply begs the question of who controls cultural production and consumption, and to what end.

Cultural reproduction

The way in which culture is transmitted through generations.

Cultures are transmitted over time and are reproduced through family, socialisation and education. Analysing the way in which **culture** is transmitted or reproduced is an important mechanism for understanding a particular culture. Tradition is a central mode by which culture is reproduced, and it has a deep psychological structure which gives it a quasi-religious status. There has been much recent work in **cultural studies** on the invention of tradition and its relationship to political change and development. Nations are formed on the basis of cultural myths of origin and national character, and one of the functions of cultural reproduction is to develop and sustain those national ideologies. At the micro-level, individuals and class cultures are reproduced in the family, and some feminists have argued that the family was the key site of the reproduction of patriarchy. Culture, like capital, is accumulated, and cultural practice and cultural reproduction exercise a powerful defining force in shaping society.

The term is used particularly in the work of innovatory French sociologist Pierre Bourdieu. He argues that the educational system effectively functions simply to reproduce the dominant culture by reproducing the distribution of **cultural capital** through the kind of cultural leadership that Antonio Gramsci described as hegemonic. What Bourdieu means by this claim is that the hierarchical systems within education ensure that those social groups with the greatest understanding of the forms in which that exclusion is exercised naturally secure the best results from the system. This is how cultural reproduction operates as a seemingly natural process of selection, and only the right sorts of people are selected. In cultural studies this is sometimes described as being a domination of the processes of signification, or control of what sorts of cultural meaning are generated in society and also what kinds of cultural practice are accorded status.

It is clear from the history of cultural studies as a discipline that for a long time working-class culture, or mass culture, was seen as intrinsically inferior to traditional culture, and this alone should alert us to the fact that we are faced with forms of cultural reproduction that reflect dominant **power** structures. Cultural judgements, like aesthetic judgements, are made from a particular point of view and reflect the group or class interests upon which they are based. It is to the credit of **postmodernism** as a theory that it has demonstrated the point that almost all cultural viewpoints can be equally valid and defensible in their own right. Cultural judgements reflect power structures and while popular culture often criticises elitest assumptions, those established ideas and practices carry a very significant psychological and ideological weight that is reinforced through cultural reproduction. What Bourdieu is getting at is the complicated process whereby there operates a psychosocial reproduction of culture and class.

Cultural studies

A mega-term that encompasses most of what used to be called the humanities.

In the beginning there was literary studies, and then there was a sociology of literature which began to include what was called 'mass' or 'popular' literature. This then developed into the study of **culture** in general and, more radically, into the study of **popular culture**, which had previously not been thought a subject worthy of attention. Cultural studies has always sought to locate the study of culture within the broader socioeconomic context, and in this it has always been a radical project, initially influenced by Marxism and later by feminist and structuralist ideas.

Under the influence of the New Left in the 1960s and 1970s, cultural studies also took a turn towards continental Marxism and its structuralist and semiotic offshoots. The work of Louis Althusser was a central influence in this shift and led to a reworking of the field which in turn led to an interest in **semiology**, the work of Roland Barthes and a more theoretically orientated analysis, rather than a concentration on the empirical discussion of working-class culture. In the 1980s, feminist criticism of the male-orientated gaze of the objects of study led to new directions in cultural studies, as did the assertion of the ethnocentric nature of cultural studies, and the field began to fragment further.

What constitutes cultural studies as a discipline or a mode of inquiry today is much debated, but it can be characterised as an interdisciplinary mode of analysis of all forms of culture which pays attention to the location of culture within wider socioeconomic frameworks. The dominance of the electronic media, and the power of consumer orientated culture, means that **identity** and politics in postmodern society are constructed in the circuits of culture that now constitute the global society; and cultural studies has become the study of global culture.

Cultural studies encompasses literary studies, media studies, **feminism**, Marxism, film studies, cultural anthropology, the study of popular culture, **subcultures**, cultural industries, questions of **race** and **ethnicity**, **psychoanalysis**, post-colonial studies, **poststructuralism** and **postmodernism**. It is worth listing the scope in this fashion merely to demonstrate the hybrid nature of the discipline, and to pose the question of whether cultural studies is now in fact the central discipline in the humanities. This opens up the question of whether cultural studies is in fact a 'cultural politics', committed to a **deconstruction** of the dominant culture, or whether it has become the institutionalised framework of general studies within a mass, postmodern, higher education marketplace.

Culturalism

An approach in cultural studies that emphasises the autonomy of culture.

An early approach within **cultural studies**, culturalism emphasised the autonomy of **culture** and its importance in reflecting the political and communal struggles of different classes. Culturalism originated both in the English critic F.R. Leavis's emphasis on the crucial shaping role of culture within **society**— what he called the civilising value—and the early work of Richard Hoggart and Raymond Williams, who sought to expand that position to working-class culture. What they were arguing was that, through an examination of the communal culture of a class—the lived experiences and cultural products—the attitudes and values of a community could be understood within their own terms, not in terms imposed from a 'high culture' perspective.

This was only radical in any sense because prior to their intervention, working-class culture was taken to be inferior and irrelevant, whereas they were arguing that it could be seen as complex, communal and as intrinsically interesting as any other culture. This was a critical step in the development of cultural studies since it brought **popular culture** within a proper intellectual framework for the first time. Williams and his colleagues also argued that popular culture should not be understood as a degraded form of entertainment that distracted the masses while acting as a conveyor belt for dominant ideology, but as a complex phenomenon whose messages were polysemous. Culturalism elevates human agency and cultural choice over a notion of culture imposed from above and, as such, is politically progressive and anti-structuralist.

In highlighting human experience—the lived—and valorising this experience, structuralists argued that culturalists fell into the trap of individualism and of ignoring the determinate structures of language and **ideology** which, for them, defined the social formation and the possible categories through which experience could be lived. The second phase of cultural studies, during which structuralist approaches became dominant, overshadowed this earlier culturalist phase and replaced the idea of lived community with that of language, structure and **discourse**.

Culture

The forms of thinking and acting in a given society.

Culture is a megaword in current **cultural studies** because so much of our understanding of social habits in contemporary society is bound up with analysing what cultural changes have occurred and why. We live in a period of human history in which change is so rapid that one generation may constitute the lifetime of a particular culture, and in which technology reinvents itself every five years, and this rate of change is accelerating. If we used a timescale of 1:1000 million years to compare the history of all human cultures to the life of the planet, we would find that human activity had existed for about one week, the industrial revolution for about one minute and postmodern culture for about 0.1 of a second, at a very generous estimate. Yet this technologically driven, global culture is what we accept as normal. We see it as a 'thick culture', one that we are part of and deeply implicated in and which is taken for granted. This tells us two very contradictory things about culture: one, that it changes very rapidly under the pressure of economic and social development; and two, that we always take it for granted as though it is natural. Culture, like religion, is society worshipping itself, and mobile phones have become the rosary beads of postmodern culture in the last five years.

The strangest fact about culture is that a very similar human species has produced the most astonishingly varied patterns and forms of culture over the centuries, cultures that have opposed one another and indulged in incredible bloodshed to validate the truth of one culture over another. Culture, we may say, seeks to explain life, but the infinite variety of cultures suggests that explanations may not always accord with either the facts or the potentiality of life to exceed the facts. Understanding culture is, then, one of the key tasks that faces most of the humanities and social sciences; defining it is almost as difficult. Thus it is that cultural studies has effectively become a discipline in its own right, centred on the many different ways that culture can be analysed. All culture is socially constructed but always seems to seek to create the illusion of a natural past, which suggests that there is a deep psychological residue to all cultural forms.

Culture is an important megaword, then, because of its flexibility and its wide use in many disciplines but, it would be fair to say, there is little agreement about its meaning. Raymond Williams famously said that it is 'one of the two or three most complicated words in the English language', and that undoubtedly relates to the fact that culture is a developing reality which changes more and more rapidly. The most straightforward example of these changes can be found in the fact that Williams has an entry in his *Keywords* for 'popular' but not for **popular culture**, a term which is today almost a disciplinary object in its own right.

Along with many other terms, 'culture' has been problematised by the structuralist and poststructuralist revolutions in thought, which have criticised many of the basic assumptions that underpinned the socialist–humanist framework within which Williams operated. In some ways the idea of culture as an expression of the better forms of human creativity underlies Williams' approach, and that assumption, too, has been regularly attacked as a historical illusion in the last two decades. Historically, culture has almost always been associated with elites and their domination of cultural practices, and it is this fundamentally political question that reappears in present-day rejections of traditional cultures. However, before deconstructing culture as an illusion, it would be worthwhile to look at the different positions that have been adopted over the definition of culture this century.

As Williams observed, the historical roots of the term go back to the idea of culturing something in the sense of growing or tending it, and this basic notion of a natural process has persisted until recently, when notions of culture as 'natural' have been overturned. At the most general level there are two broad definitions which take up the different uses of the term. First, there is culture as the artistic, linguistic and literary forms of **civilisation**; the intellectual and spiritual expressions of thought, art and literature. Second, there is culture as the much broader idea of 'way of life', the description of all of the symbolic and material aspects of human life, language and behaviour, including attitudes, artefacts, beliefs, sciences, customs and habits. In other words the complex whole of non-biological activity. This definition relates culture to material production.

Both of these definitions are very broad, and can endlessly be broken down into smaller subdivisions—such as popular culture, high culture and class culture—but they represent the fundamental axis along which the debate is carried on. An even broader definition would be to say that culture is the organised forms of the social production and reproduction of meaning, knowledge and values; the totality of forms of activity that differentiate human societies from others. Put like this there doesn't seem to be much difference between culture and **society**, whereas of course there is a considerable difference, which is why the definitions that accentuate the 'meaning/signifying' aspects of culture are probably the most important.

One of the central difficulties about culture is that it seems natural to the individual, whereas culture is in fact a man-made artefact which has always been subjected to change and development. The more established a culture is, the more natural it feels and the less its socially constructed nature is apparent. Understanding culture then becomes difficult because culture is always bound up with education, **power** and forms of class consciousness and **ideology**. It is probably the case that it is easier to analyse culture in its more specific manifestations, like popular culture or punk culture, and that overarching theories of culture, like **structuralism**, posit such grand generalisations that they fail to conceptualise the 'lived-ness' of culture. Williams always emphasised the experiential, lived-in quality of culture and its contradictory political nature, which contrasts fairly sharply with many structuralist definitions of culture which define it as a monolithic concept. The definition of 'high' and 'popular' (or low) culture is a useful way of historically separating out the different approaches to understanding culture, since it highlights the implied historical sense of culture as 'cultivated' or superior.

Raymond Williams (1981) defined culture as consisting of three related elements: a 'lived' element, a 'documentary' element and an 'ideal' element. There is a more anthropological feel to Williams' approach to culture, and this is positive in that anthropology had always had a neutral and non-evaluative approach to the complexities of culture. Cultural studies took up this more anthropological approach and began to consider all cultures as intrinsically interesting, rather than comparing an ennobling high culture to a debased low culture. Williams' definition also incorporates the interconnectedness of different forms of culture, an approach which echoes that of Antonio Gramsci, who first looked at the ways in which elite, mass and traditional cultures were dynamically interrelated and always being contested.

By the lived element of culture, Williams is referring to 'whole ways of life': the patterns, forms and structures of everyday life that form a coherent whole and which cultural studies examines in looking at youth culture, ethnic groups, **subcultures**, audiences and new social movements. The 'documentary' aspects of culture relate to the way in which meaning and culture are framed and communicated in society, particularly in the media, entertainment, film, literature and any other systems of communication that record and transmit cultural meanings. The 'ideal' element of culture refers to what was traditionally seen as the proper study of criticism and analysis: the art, literature and elite creative work of the dominant culture.

The question in literary and cultural studies became one of estimating the value of these kinds of cultural artefacts: did they have status because of their intrinsic qualities, or because they were the officially sanctioned culture of elite groups? The answer to this question is rather more complicated than sometimes seems the case, since dismissing, as many Marxists did, all **bourgeois** art and literature for ideological reasons means throwing out the Shakespeare with the monarchist poet laureate. Cultural studies brought to the fore all of these questions of how to evaluate different kinds of culture, and has persistently stressed the socially constructed dimensions of culture, and the difficulties of analysing cultural formations that are in a constant state of flux.

Cyberpunk

A politico-aesthetic movement that utilises technology and music to create new forms.

This is a very recent term that obviously derives from **cyberspace** and also from the rebellious punk movement of the 1970s and 1980s. Cyberpunk is difficult to define because, rather like punk itself, it is as much an attitude as a set of ideas. It can best be described as the coming together of the world of high technology and the low world of underground music and rock rebellion. Cyberpunk is an urban postmodern reaction to the uniformity of technological order, as well as being a transgression of the **binary oppositions** of nature and science, organic and inorganic, male and female, human and machine.

Like the figure of the **cyborg**, the cyberpunk claims an indeterminate identity and a free-floating space in which to operate. Cyberpunk recycles the objects and ideas of the dominant culture in a blasphemous remix of subcultural memories and a technological subversion of control. Cyberpunk includes 'hackers' as well as 'neurotechnology', the street as the site of recycling and the technosphere as the possibility of global regeneration. In all, cyberpunk is an anarchic expression of the destruction of all boundaries, and a self-mutilating freedom that subverts and rejects the **body**.

Cyberspace

The virtual world made possible by new digital and telecommunications technologies, especially the Internet and interactive communication.

This is a term that has a very recent history and yet has already so entered everyday usage that its meaning is taken for granted. Cyberspace is a potential or virtual space where humans interact through computers, creating a new dimension of communication, interaction and new forms of **knowledge**. The Internet is seen as being the primary region of cyberspace, although cyberspace also has other spatial and aesthetic dimensions. Quite fittingly, the term was coined by William Gibson who saw cyberspace as a kind of hallucinatory new dimension where information, **virtual reality** and public communication blended in a new form. Gibson apparently said later that the term was a 'cut-up word', an invention to describe a new mode of communication. The term is already used without qualification or criticism, itself an indication of how fast the communication cultural revolution is occurring.

According to the most optimistic proponents of cyberspace, it is producing a new kind of global mind and giving rise to the most revolutionary change in socio-cultural life since the invention of the printing press. In the form of the Internet, cyberspace is clearly revolutionising the way that society operates, particularly in terms of commerce, although whether it is another dimension of **culture** remains to be seen.

Critics of ideas about cyberspace point out that it is used as a term within a cultural **ecology** of new technology: this means that while there are discussions about how people use the Internet, there is little concrete discussion of the actual technologies and their historical development. Technology is immersed in mysticism, a charge that was often levelled against Marshall McLuhan's optimistic analysis of the 'global village' in his seminal work *The Medium Is the Massage* (1967). The question 'What is a virtual community?' brings home this new strain of positivism: the term 'virtual community' is constantly used in a self-congratulatory fashion without any clarification. **Virtual reality** may be a metaphor for a new cultural dimension, but computer industries are tightly organised forms of economic and social power, and the relationship between the two is still being theorised.

Cyborg

A creature (cybernetic organism) of the post-gender world.

This term was originally coined by the defence and science industries to refer to hybrid systems that incorporated organic and technological elements. Donna Haraway gave the term a feminist inflection in her ground-breaking 1985 article 'A manifesto for cyborgs: science, technology, and socialist feminism in the 1980s'. Haraway argues that the cyborg is a figure that represents a way to think past the naturalised categories of **race**, **class** and **gender** and to rethink the impact of technology on social relations and, in particular, gender relations. This is to say, the cyborg can be seen as prefigurative reality in which the possibilites of a utopian technological future can be imagined.

The cyborg has entered **popular culture** through science fiction and film, and has already inspired many myths about the development and dissolution of human/science boundaries. Haraway uses the idea of the cyborg to posit a new form of hybrid **subjectivity** that is outside the constraints of existing social realities, the potentiality of which occupies a space she calls 'cyberfeminism'. Instead of the organic, whole and natural female self, she argues that women should seize the possibilities inherent in new technology, in networks, to become a 'post-modern collective and personal self'. The cyborg is meant to be representative of a post-gender world.

There are those who view this optimism about technological possibility as being misplaced, seeing in technology the threat of controlling women's bodies as much as the promise of liberating them. The body is everywhere changing, however, and the prefigurative form of the cyborg suggests ways of moving beyond the naturalism that dominates much of our thinking.

Deconstruction

The practice of exposing metaphysics as historical illusion; taking apart hierarchical oppositions of western metaphysics.

The idea of deconstruction and its application is seminal to all **cultural studies** over the last 20 years, both because of its attack on **structuralism** but also because of its magpie-like attitude to all theoretical discourses, its chameleon-like ability to change its nature as it develops and its passage from obscure theory to acceptance in **popular culture**. Like **postmodernism**, the term 'deconstruct' has entered the lexicon of popular cultural journalism that now espouses theory as a kind of lifestyle. Its indeterminacy is its strength, and its playfulness fits perfectly with the insouciance of postmodern paradigms. According to Jacques Derrida, it is not a question of abandoning philosophy but of borrowing from the traditions of philosophy the means to deconstruct that tradition. One is therefore outside of, but working within, philosophy in order to prove its endless delusion of absolute meaning.

Deconstruction is the dominant trend in **poststructuralism**. It is also a philosophical method, a mode of literary analysis and, according to some, a nihilistic end point of self-indulgent literary theory. Derrida coined the term in his 1967 key text *Of Grammatology* and has been developing it ever since. Before Derrida, people read texts to understand their point of view; now, after Derrida (AD) we 'deconstruct' texts in order to show that all texts meet the same fate, which is that of self-contradiction. At its most simple level, deconstruction is an approach which claims that it is fundamentally wrong to assume that a text has a fixed meaning which can be recovered through a straightforward reading. It is in literary theory that this approach has had the most influence, particularly in the United States, although it has also filtered into the work and writing of many other disciplines. There are always two basic moves in deconstruction: firstly, the critique and reversal of **binary oppositions** that hierarchically structure the object of critique, Derrida's example of 'speech' over 'writing' being the most infamous. This move demonstrates the **logocentrism** which guarantees these hierachical binary oppositions through the idea of presence, or centre. The second move is to look at the dispersal of meaning along the lines of what Derrida calls **difference**, or the instability of meaning.

Derrida's first step in grammatology (which means 'theory of writing') is to analyse the way in which he sees great philosophers as forever denouncing writing as being inferior to speech, which is favoured as being more redolent of human meaning. Philosophers may give precedence to speech, although that is debatable, but Derrida's own view is certainly not clear. His is more a theory of metaphysics than a theory of writing. Philosophers' concern with writing—the dead, dispersed permanent record of metaphysical illusion—is proof of their delusions and their desire to indulge in the metaphysics of certainty. This 'myth-of-presence' (what Derrida also calls **logocentrism**) is there for Derrida in the deadness of language, in the inert traces of writing as opposed to speech.

Deconstruction is about exposing the falsity of metaphysics, of the idea of fixed, centred meaning and of the mythical presences that purport to give sanction to the illusion of meaning. Since meaning is seen as being guaranteed by the illusion of an external presence—whether it be God, the author, myths of origin or whatever—then it is similarly the case that writing, or texts, carry a similar illusion as to the making of meaning. The elision from logocentrism to textual criticism is difficult to justify since an author may well be presenting not an absolutist claim of knowledge but a specific textual rendition of the undecidability of specific meaning. In fact, many novels are precisely about that undecidability, and may even have a deconstructive aim themselves. Forcing such texts through the deconstructive mill appears to replace the illusion of the author with the disillusion of the critic.

Deconstruction historically developed out of structuralism, and its basis in linguistic theory is obvious at every turn, hence its description as a philosophy of **poststructuralism**. If we see deconstruction as a reaction to the limitations of structuralist oppositions and the inflexible patterns of analysis that structuralism led to, it makes more sense. Where structuralists saw meaning as fixed in the position of the sign, Derrida sees this only as a displacement, a deferment. At the level of language, Derrida wants to escape from the system that imprisons the process of representation, but his debt to that system is always there, which is one of the many conundrums of deconstruction. Deconstruction has, however, one form of escape from the system, which is the claim that meaning can never be fixed, is always deferred, just as a deconstructive analysis of a text will never arrive at a final definition.

As if to counter this undecidability and endless transformation of potentiality, deconstruction advocates a close reading of the text, a painstaking shifting of its flaws, and attempts to create meaning, to kick over the traces of its own complicity in illusion. Such reading inevitably finds the contradiction in the text's attempts to pass itself off as coherent, and the marginalised, repressed elements of the text's hierarchy of oppositions is brought into play. The constant movement within deconstruction between levels of meaning and discourse, emphasising the marginalised and the repressed, and the open-endedness of the text have led one critic to remark that deconstruction is no more than 'a careful teasing out of warring forces of signification within the text'. This is a position that it is difficult not to agree with, although critics are more sceptical about deconstruction's claims to rewriting the entire history of philosophy and thought. However, even when deconstructive analysis of a literary text is considered, it rapidly becomes apparent that the endless play of signification and the 'warring forces' are always everywhere remarkably similar. Like old-fashioned Marxist readings of classical texts, one starts with a complex narrative and ends with the same old story: a fishy bit of **ideology** dangling from the deconstructive hook.

Desire

Naughty, but nice.

Although Sigmund Freud developed the psychological concept of desire, physical desire had long been accepted as a phenomenon. Freud assumed that because women did not have penises, they would automatically desire them (penis envy) and, if they could not have them, they would castrate the men who did (castration complex). In Freudian thought desire resides in the subconscious, which often influences our actions.

In postmodern thought 'desire' has come to represent all levels of libidinal drive and such drives are seen to subvert the rational mind. Michel Foucault argued that acceptable sexual desire in society had been limited to heterosexuality within the sanctity of marriage. Throughout the late twentieth century, much political activism targeted desire, for example, the women's liberation movement and the gay rights lobby.

Determinism

Reducing events to their basic causes.

Determinism reduces events in the world to a few causal factors and disregards the effect of individual autonomous actions and of complex causal chains. For example, biological determinism argues that physical characteristics, together with population patterns, are solely responsible for shaping society.

Diaspora

A term that refers to a relational network; the connections of dispersal.

This historical term was originally used to describe the experience of the Jewish people after they were scattered following

107

the Roman domination of Palestine in the first century AD. The term refers to their common experience and connection after being forced into exile. This experience of ethnic or cultural groups being dispersed or scattered has been repeated throughout history, particularly during the periods of **colonialism** and **imperialism**. Thus the term has come to be used in studies of **race** and **ethnicity** to describe and discuss this experience of dislocation and the ways in which cultural affinities are maintained when groups are dispersed, as in slavery.

Diaspora does not just mean dispersal but also alludes to the fact that violence and threat have historically been constitutive of the experience of the dispersed. The identity that is shared in the experience of the diaspora is, then, not just a community of interests but a dynamic of suffering and deprivation which is a powerful political force that insists on memory as a means of dealing with the present. This kind of experience has been shared by many ethnic groups, including Irish, African, Caribbean, Chinese and Filipino, among others. The fact of dispersal, of discontinuity, tends to produce a symbolism that exaggerates belonging and creates an idealised illusion of homeland, a sense of essential **identity** which is also displaced. Rather than a settled 'national' identity, the diasporic experience is one of change, threat, hope and nostalgia, reflecting an unsettled community that has to constantly rebuild itself—the very model for society today.

The black diaspora, or what Paul Gilroy (1993) has called the Black Atlantic diaspora, created through slavery, and the Jewish diaspora, reinforced through the holocaust, have been the most extreme examples of social and cultural dislocation in the last two centuries. Their experience has been somewhat mirrored, however, by the post-World War II exodus of the Palestinians.

Difference

A Saussurian term expressing the belief that language is created solely through the use of comparison and contrast between word and concept.

Difference reigns supreme in critical thought at the present time, so much so that it has taken on a quasi-religious status in much cultural thought. Difference is a megaword with a difference, since at its simplest level it merely refers to the fact that things are different, or are experienced differently, or are not identical. This simple definition has given rise to an astonishing array of variegated meanings.

Uses of the term spread through **cultural studies** from its original meaning in structural linguistics, in the work of Ferdinand de Saussure, through **feminism**, literary and media studies to poststructuralist and deconstructionist philosophies, acquiring more and more complex layers of meaning as it unfolded. Difference, specifically sexual difference, has also been a keyword in feminist theory over the last two decades.

Difference is expressed most obviously in **binary oppositions** to the thing that the subject is not, like light/dark, dead/alive, sane/insane, etc. Saussure argues that binary oppositions are essential to the production of meaning and that difference is therefore an important element in understanding language and culture. This may not seem immediately obvious, but what Saussure is saying is that within language—or, more properly, the structural relations which make up the system of language— the production of meaning is made up by presences and absences: the sign is what it is because it is not the other elements that could be used from the system. For example, to say 'dog' is not to say 'cat' or, to put it another way, 'dog' means 'not-cat' rather than positively 'dog'. Thus for Saussure 'there are only differences without positive terms' in language. So difference is somehow an absolutely fundamental principle of all language and since the structuralists compare culture to language then difference is a central principle in **culture**.

Awareness of difference was taken up at the textual level, at the ideological level and at the level of **gender** and culture. This led on to the question of **identity** and difference, which has also become a central argument in recent cultural studies, and to the centrality of difference in feminist studies. In literary and cultural studies the pursuit of difference looked at the structure of oppositions within a text, the relationships between the kinds of binary structures that gave meaning to a literary work: the opposition between the country and the city, the goodie and the baddie in westerns, or the mother and the whore, etc.

It has regularly been claimed, however, that there is an imbalance between the opposing terms of binary oppositions, and that there is always a dominant term. So literary texts began to be examined in terms not only of difference but also of what was suppressed: the not-said of oppositions that give rise to dominant readings and cultural interpretations. However, structuralist readings of texts were dominated by the concern with difference, which elevated the dualistic nature of all thinking to a universal principle, an approach which was heavily criticised by Jacques Derrida and the deconstructionists.

Difference, as used by Derrida, combines the general sense of difference and of deferment: it is the way in which meaning is permanently deferred, is unstable and potential. In this it is the opposite of the fixed meaning of metaphysics, the **logocentrism** that maintains the fiction of absolute meaning. This deferment, displacement, delay, postponement, impossibility of meaning that Derrida endlessly rehearses at one level seems exactly like the binary opposite of the absolute meaning that he denounces, thus seemingly imprisoning him in the very system he is always attempting to escape. He has fairly regularly reworked this concept of difference, which seems logical enough given his commitment to the falsity of fixed meaning, but this can make writing about it unproductive. The obvious question would seem to be whether or not there is some position on meaning which is somewhere between total indeterminacy and absolute meaning.

In all fields of study difference is counterposed to **identity**, or essentialism or foundationalism, so that it is taken for granted that difference is a productive term. Stressing difference and plurality is all very well but there then comes a time, we may say in the last instance, when some communal identity or sameness might be politically useful in constructing community or social movements. Posing essentialist identities or fixed meanings as the enemy against which difference elevates itself sometimes seems no more than the endless poststructuralist insistence on deferral and fragmentation; men and women are different but they seem to use exactly the same language of difference. Furthermore, conceptualising all social realities as difference seems to elide the questions of **class**, economic power and **cultural capital** that still seem to determine much of what passes for social reality.

Discourse

A body of ideas, an ensemble of social practices.

This is a term that led a long and uneventful life with a generally accepted meaning until French philosopher Michel Foucault turned it on its head in the 1960s and made it into a central idea in his analysis of history and ideas. Unlike many concepts in the humanities, this idea emerged in its Foucauldian form almost without predecessors, which is to say that it was a radical switch of attention from theories of **ideology**, of **agency**, of **class** and of **gender** struggle. In its traditional, historical sense, a discourse was simply a speech or writing on a particular subject. There are many historical examples of a 'discourse on morals, manners', etc. but, after Foucault's appropriation of the term, 'discourse' was to become a central concept in cultural and gender studies. Discourse is similar to ideology in that it refers to the ways in which people make sense of the social world and their place in it, but Foucault argues that it is a radically different way of thinking about how the social functions. Discourse is 'the complex of signs and practices which organises social existence and social reproduction'.

The meaning of a particular kind of speech in discourse was taken over by Foucault as he was very interested in the way that language was used, and how its usage affected both the speaker and the listener. Many disciplines, from sociology to literary and cultural studies, were at the same time developing an interest in the way that language was used, because it was increasingly felt that communication was the key to understanding how **culture** and **society** worked. At its most basic, the notion of 'discourse' simply refers to a unit of speech that is greater than a sentence or a simple utterance: it is more a whole way of speech. For Foucault, it is also a historically situated material practice that produces power relations, and this is where it differs from traditional notions of ideology.

Foucault dispenses with what earlier thinkers like Louis Althusser would have called ideology, or a set of ideas and presumptions about a particular field, like medicine, and replaces it with the notion of a discourse. For Foucault, a discourse is a 'large body of statements' governed by an internal set of rules which limit and define how those statements are used in society. The discourse of medicine might, in an earlier epoch, have been called the 'medical discipline', implying both the whole body of knowledge and the way that it is used in the medical field. What Foucault is arguing is that all of the 'strategic possibilities' of the way that discourse operates, or in other words all of the hidden assumptions and practices that make up the conscious and unconscious patterns of operating within a discipline, are best characterised by thinking of it as discourse, rather than a discipline. Foucault also talks about what he calls a 'discursive formation', which seems to be much the same thing as a discourse but perhaps with a stronger institutional or theoretical base. The law, or the legal system, is a fairly obvious discursive formation, with its own language, rules, conventions, modes of behaviour, history, aims and objectives (Foucault, 1971; 1972).

Foucault wrote about the discourses of sexuality and madness, and of the ways that ideas are represented and reproduced in a discourse, governing who says what about the nature of illness, its conventions and regularities. Discourse is **power** for Foucault, and the modes of saying are always constitutive of power relations at the local level. Society, Foucault argues, has particular procedures for the production and organisation of discourses, and for the regulation of their transmission, selection and redistribution. Understanding these discursive practices is what cultural and historical study should pay attention to.

So for Foucault, discourse is this 'group of statements in so far as they belong to a discursive formation', (Foucault, 1972) but this keeps hedging around the question of whether discourse is all there is: that is to say, whether discourse constitutes the world. Elsewhere Foucault says that discourse mediates between the ideal and the material world, that it is a set of relations, of regularities, which produce social relations.

Division of labour

Who gets to do what.

The division of labour is an apparently neutral term, but it has come to represent the unequal allocation of tasks within societies. Certain groups in **society** are seen to be more at risk of exploitation than others, for example, women, children and people from racial minorities.

Industrial societies have complex divisions of labour because of the variety of commodities produced and services provided, requiring a range of skills. The roles people perform greatly affect their share of **power**, wealth, and status.

Dominant/Residual/Emergent

The factions within cultures that are always in a state of conflict.

This is a related set of terms that was used by Raymond Williams in discussing the formations of **culture**, and which incorporated Antonio Gramsci's ideas about **hegemony** and cultural struggle. What Williams was talking about was the fact that representing culture as a fixed, static set of relations, as **structuralism** did, was to ignore the reality that culture and **society** are in a constant state of flux. Williams was also criticising the **Frankfurt School**'s approach to culture in which it was seen as being a one-dimensional industry which dominated everything within society. There is a dominant cultural order, Williams argues, but within it there exist both elements of traditional culture and elements of new oppositional cultures—all of which can be in conflict with the dominant order.

It is perhaps interesting that Williams was writing within the confines of British culture, a culture that carries deep traditional imagery which often conflicts with the commercial realities of **popular culture**, as well as with the radical cultures like punk. The cultural theory of **postmodernism**, that all such culture becomes part of the hyperreal, of endless signification, seems to iron out the contradictions and oppositions of living culture just as much as the reductionism of many Marxist approaches. Emergent cultures, like new social movements, similarly pose powerful oppositions to the dominant culture, and conflict with it.

Doxa

A broader term than ideology, meaning something close to common-sense or everyday assumptions.

Pierre Bourdieu's sociology of everyday life, and of how **culture** functions in **society**, is a complex and specific analysis of empirical reality that takes a stand against the over-generalising tendencies of **postmodernism**, and of its claim that reality has simply become the simulacrum of itself. His notion of the doxa is an attempt to describe in specific terms how the habits and characteristics of everyday life are built up in socialisation and remain with the individual throughout their life-career, albeit subject to change and development.

Doxa refers to the taken for granted, naturalised patterns of behaviour and assumptions that operate in a given field of practice. Bourdieu argues that these patterns of behaviour are akin to common sense, but they are not simply **ideology**, or even unconscious, as Louis Althusser would have it, but patterns of behaviour embedded in the practice itself, even in the body. The concept is similar to Antonio Gramsci's notion of 'common sense' in that it refers to an encrusted form of thinking which carries the residues of popular ideas, the stone-age patterns of everyday **appropriation** of the world and a measure of experience that is both viable and anachronistic. Rather like peasant culture, the doxa is both deeply traditional, effectively reproduced and reactionary in its presentation of men and women.

Ecology

An extraordinarily complicated term that refers to the whole of the planet and its environment.

Ecology and the related term 'environmentalism' refer to a recent concern and understanding of the relationship between humans and the physical environment in which they live. The Greek origins of the term refer to 'the whole house' or the combination of science and nature and it is to this holistic vision that the term returns in order to overcome the **culture/nature** split that is so endemic in modern **society**.

Concern with the environment is clear in the anti-industrialism of the Romantic reaction in the nineteenth century, but it only became a political force in the post-nuclear age, developing out of the radical student movements of the 1960s. Based on a concern for the environment and drawing on holistic concepts of man's place in nature, the ecology movement has created a new form of politics, a 'green' reread-ing of political activism and social aims. The ecological approach argues for a 'humans-in-nature' understanding of social development, rather than an approach which separates out politics, industrialism or economics.

The ecology movement is extremely broad and encompasses eastern philosophies, eco-feminism, indigenous movements, post-colonial critics of western globalisation, anti-capitalist anarchists and new age theorists. There is a theoretical approach known as 'deep ecology' which posits a powerful natural balance and force in the world which, when disturbed, leads to inevitable environmental catastrophe. There is an idea of nature within these formulations that, as in eastern philos-ophies, posits nature as female, as the 'mother-earth'. Whatever the difficulties of these positions, it is clear that the ecological critique of unlimited economic growth is beginning to be widely accepted, and that alternative methods of production and economic management are urgently needed.

Economic rationalism *see* Neo-liberalism, Thatcherism

Ecriture feminine

A form of women's writing; a potential mode of writing.

This is a term which has its roots in French **feminism**, but also in the history of radical feminist theory, which has always seen the female body as the site of a different mode of thinking, always repressed by the phallocentric order. There has been a tradition of criticism which has claimed that the **power** of forms of male thought, as expressed in language itself, has consistently suppressed the reality of the modes of thinking of the feminine, and écriture feminine is the term used for that suppressed women-centred thinking and writing. It is most associated with the French thinker Hélène Cixous, and she has clearly said that écriture feminine is as much a possibility as a clearly defined reality, but that it marked the space where a feminist practice of writing would develop. It denotes a type of writing, a style, a feeling and form of discourse different to modes of male writing—it is not intimately related to biology, but to both the mother and the mother–child relationship. This rather complex idea comes out of conceptions of the formation of the gendered subject, the role of language in that formation and the way that language inscribes masculinity and femininity. Referring to the mother–child relationship is to draw attention to the point of development before the child acquires 'conventional language' and thereby **culture**, and in which pre-intonational communication lays down a deeper bond than that of communicative language. The term is mostly used in literary and feminist criticism, but it has a wider sociological sense in relation to an understanding of the representations of masculinity/femininity in modern culture.

Ecriture feminine claims to go beyond the **binary oppositions** of patriarchal logic, to create in the space of writing a **deconstruction** of the established oppositions of theoretical and literary discourses and to replace them with an experimental form of femininity. The materiality of language is emphasised and often a lyrical, utopian strain is found in the expression of feminine **difference** and the articulation of **desire**. The question in literary studies, of course, is whether an écriture feminine exists, or whether it is either an essentialist fallacy or a utopian collapsing of style, body and **discourse** into a type of writing that reproduces marginality.

Empiricism

The idea that knowledge is based on experience.

This is an idea that has a long history in philosophy, and relates to the empirical study of things that are observed from first-hand experience. Since the rise of **structuralism**, **semiotics** and, latterly, **postmodernism**, the idea that reality can be experienced first hand has been mostly abandoned in favour of the view that reality is constructed through language and **culture**. 'Experience' is the key category of empiricism and the notion has been heavily criticised as an untheorised imaginary relation to the real. Empircists argue that **knowledge** is based on observation and only theoretical knowledge which can be verified against empirical observation is valid. Theory must be deduced from empirical observation. It is claimed that theoretical principles can be separated from empirical observations and that therefore complete objectivity can be built up. This approach claims that observing the world 'as it is' is a straightforward, uncomplicated matter and that one simply has to report the facts.

Theorists from Marx onwards have challenged this approach, pointing out that most views of the world carry a **bias**—whether conscious or unconscious—which distorts what is seen. Feminism has been very critical of empiricist approaches since, it is argued, they are often inherently masculine in their assumed neutrality. For a long time empiricist scientists claimed that women were unable to compete in sport, that black people were genetically inferior, that men were naturally highly sexed and women passive, and so on. The point is that what was observed was what was already believed and the 'facts' were constructions of those theoretical positions. It is not possible to separate the observable world from the position of the person observing it, nor to report on the world without already having a position about how it functions. Empiricism has an important ideological function, it is, for example an important defence in the claims of the media to be neutral, since they claim merely to report the world as it is.

Encoding/Decoding

The process by which meaning is constructed and understood in messages.

This definition goes back to a moment in cultural studies during the 1970s when **semiotics** was beginning to have an impact and a one-dimensional view of **culture** was being rejected in favour of a more complex, polysemous, view of the media. In Stuart Hall's article on encoding/decoding, which was very influential in this period, he argues that the process of communication has to be considered as both the construction and **deconstruction** of messages, not as a way-one flow. Encoding refers to the way in which media messages are constructed and produced, whereas decoding refers to the way in which they are received and understood, a process that can involve negotiated meanings and even oppositional readings.

Hall is making the fairly obvious point that whatever the intended message of a media communication, audiences can interpret it in very different ways depending on their age, **class**, **gender**, cultural background, etc. To put it another way, we can say that the media have to work at winning over, defining and dominating the process of cultural communication, and that oppositional ideas and viewpoints always exist outside the defining framework of the media. This is not to deny that the media are powerful institutions in society and almost universally act in ways supportive of the dominant ideology, but simply to reinforce the point that most media messages are polysemous.

End of philosophy

The idea that traditional philosophy no longer has any relevance or validity.

Radical postmodern theories claim that the traditional modes of philosophy, particularly analytic and scientific philosophy, are irrelevant as they no longer have anything to say about the construction of reality. Based on the critical relativism of theories deriving from Friedrich Nietzsche, Michel Foucault and Martin Heidegger, end of philosophy approaches deconstruct the delusions of western metaphysics. These approaches are still very contentious.

Enlightenment

A historical period when rationality, reason and equality were seen as important ideas.

The Enlightenment refers to a period in the seventeenth and eigtheenth centuries during which the foundations of modern science and technology, together with rational and liberal ideologies of progress and development, were laid down. Beginning with a critique of the divine right of kings and of religion itself, Enlightenment thinkers developed a critique of **society** and a theory of a rational, ordered world. Many link the rise of Enlightenment reason with the work of René Descartes, who proposed rationality as the basic credo of all humanities and individualism as its central motif, however Enlightenment thought was fundamentally social in character rather than philosophical. It was a Europe-wide movement that drew on many sources and encompassed philosophy, political theory, literature and the beginnings of sociological thought.

Enlightenment thinking has to be seen in the context of the mythical and reactionary religious thought that preceded it, and the feudal social structures to which it was opposed, not in the light of postmodern concerns with millennial relativism. The French and American revolutions owed a great deal to the liberating and critical thought of the Enlightenment and, in particular, the political ideas of equality and freedom before the law for all individuals, whatever their social origin. In fact to believe in the innate possibility of reason and goodness in all men, and women, was itself a somewhat revolutionary idea at the time, especially as women were not universally seen as being equal to men. Internationally, thinkers like Thomas Paine, author of *The Rights of Man*, John Locke, David Hume, François Voltaire and Denis Diderot, were central to the movement.

In France there was a large and significant group of thinkers who came to represent the ideal of the Enlightenment. Known as the the Encyclopaedists, they set out to lay down the totality of all human knowledge at the time, based on rational principles, and to examine its practical application, particularly for social theory. This was to be the greatest encyclopaedia of all time and the forerunner to the Age of Reason but, as we know, this was a slightly over-optimistic view of the development of history. The great German thinker and poet Johann Goethe saw both the possibility of 'reason' as the future of mankind and the delusions of grandeur that it might entail, and in the figure of Faust he gives us one of the **iconic** emblems of that period. Reason, secularism, universalism, science and empirical thought were the intellectual tools with which the Enlightenment was driven forward, and the social and political thought it produced can only be seen as progressive in its historical context. If we now deconstruct the Enlightenment to rewrite it as another history, this merely tells us about our reconstruction of the past as documentary present.

Some thinkers have argued that the development of rationality, of Enlightenment reason, has turned into what is called 'instrumental reason' or rationalisation, and that this has led to a repressive form of society. This seems to confuse the belief in reason and freedom that the Enlightenment stood for with the outcome of the development of modernity and bureaucratic capitalist society. Whether the two are connected seems a very open question. This kind of anti-Enlightenment argument has been taken up by postmodernists, who rail against the repressive hypothesis of reason and elevate fragmentation, the 'local' and the micro-political. Jürgen Habermas, on the other hand, argues that the Enlightenment was more a critical frame of mind than a rigid set of doctrines and that therefore it does not make sense to be anti-Enlightenment.

Enonce/enonciation

The distinction between speaking and the effects of that act.

It is argued in linguistic theory that this distinction is an important one that refers to the act of speaking, or enunciation, and its results. Roland Barthes and Umberto Eco use this distinction in fairly similar ways, which basically refer to the difference between the act of speaking and the consequences of that speech, but it was French linguist Emile Beneviste who theorised the difference between the enonce (a statement free of context) and the enonciation (a statement tied to context).

Umberto Eco renders these terms as 'sentence' and 'utterance', which helps to distinguish the thing said from the act of saying it, but does not necessarily illuminate its importance. The accepted interpretation is that the actual, time-bound act of making the statement can be very different from the result of that statement, a result which flies off out of the control of the subject making it. In a world in which language is seen as a totalising, independent reality, this distinction draws attention to how a statement can be addressed to another subject, or rather abstractly be aimed at the universe of meaning in which words communicate.

Episteme

The dominant mode of organising thought at a given historical time.

This is another term that comes out of the work of the philosopher/historian Michel Foucault and which really needs to be read in the context of his whole theoretical approach. At its most basic, Foucault uses it to mean the generally accepted mode of getting and organising **knowledge** in a particular era, such as the medieval, classic or modern eras. An episteme acts as the overarching organising principle of the era, uniting the different discourses within it. Thus science, law, medicine, history, etc. are seen as being united through an underlying structure of assumptions about how knowledge is produced and used. This generalised structure of knowledge is the framework in which the different discourses operate, thus giving an overall coherence to the formations of knowledge.

Foucault's work historicises different epistemes and seems to suggest that the functioning of the episteme is the dominant factor in the order of things, this being a somewhat idealist notion of determination and a direct reversal of the Marxist approach which claims that the economic **base** determines the **superstructure**. At the same time, this model of epistemic coherence is clearly structuralist in its insistence on abstract laws, and de-historicising in its retrospective reduction of all forms of knowledge to one pattern. In *The Order of Things* (1970), Foucault says that the episteme is:

> The total set of relations that unite, at a given period, the discursive practices that give rise to epistemological figures, sciences and possibly formalized systems ... it is the totality of relations that can be discovered for a given period, between the sciences when one analyses them at the level of discursive regularities.

Foucault's notion of the episteme is useful in bringing into the open the fact that at different periods different ideas are accepted as universals, but the gains thus made are somewhat dissipated by the structuralist insistence on regularities and coherence. In discussing the modern order, Foucault argues that it is based on the humanist assumptions centred on 'man' the individual, and this informs psychology, sociology, literature, history, myth and so on in this period. This 'modern' period, however, is often described by others as being dominated by abstract science, industrialisation and the emergence of the masses, both theoretically and politically, so the question of how this episteme of the humanities is dominant is rather an open one. There is also the question of what relationship an episteme has to either **ideology** or to what Raymond Williams called a 'structure of feeling'.

At one level Foucault claims that an episteme governs what is knowledge or truth in a particular era, but it is not clear whether this function is simply a reflection of dominant trends or an epistemological fact. The term has gained considerable currency within certain academic discourses, however, possibly because it adds a certain scientificity to the humanities discourses which are so mired in conflict and uncertainty.

Epistemology

A theory of knowledge, of how we know, perceive, feel and understand.

Theories of how we come to acquire or develop **knowledge** about the world underpin most cultural theory, whether covertly or explicitly. For example, scientific approaches claim that we can have objective knowledge of the world, whereas many post-modern theories reject that epistemology altogether, claiming that the world is a constructed relativity. The sense of **self** and of subjective knowledge are also important areas of debate in epistemology. **Empiricism**, or the belief that all knowledge is based on experience, on observation, is an epistemology. All theoretical approaches to understanding the world are based on an epistemological standpoint.

Essentialism

The belief that people, groups or objects have fixed, innate characteristics.

This is a term that, like **reductionism**, carries an overtone of accusation. To take an overtly essentialist position on a topic in cultural studies today is tantamount to declaring oneself a believer in unicorns, or witches. This is not to deny that most essentialist arguments are, however, fundamentally flawed, if not illusory. The idea that men are inherently more rational than women, for example, is an essentialist belief that was firmly held for many centuries. An essentialist belief, then, is one that posits a universal essence, an attribute that is unchanging, to people or cultural groups, or cultural forms.

The problem with essentialism in **cultural studies** is that many ideas in **popular culture**, or common-sense ideologies in everyday life, assume certain essential characteristics in many areas like the male/female divide, racial or ethnic characteristics. In discussing **identity** many writers assume certain essential shared characteristics, particularly feminist writers, some of whom posit an essential feminine, or feminine writing. Of course if there is an essential feminine, there must be an essential masculine, which might suggest that political progress was improbable, if not impossible. One woman's essentialism cannot be another man's **relativism**, and this is the central problem of all essentialist approaches: they argue for fixed elements which give a credibility to the argument but then lock it into that position.

The attraction of an essentialist argument is that the basics of the position are assumed to be self-evident, so they do not need to be discussed. **Ideology** often operates through essentialist statements, as does the particular ideological approach of the New Right and economic rationalist models. An appeal to an essentialist truth, like the operation of free markets, has a deep appeal to many people because it offers an answer in a world of confusion and subjective disarray, and this appeal operates at all levels of human appropriation of reality. Despite all the arguments of cultural studies, feminist and **queer** theory, essentialist positions about masculinity and femininity remain very powerful in popular culture and thought.

Ethics

A branch of philosophy which investigates morality and human behaviour.

Connections between ethics, **society** and politics have been recognised since the time of Aristotle and Plato. In a formal sense, ethics are concerned with the rightness and wrongness of actions, the motives which prompt them, the agents who perform them and the consequences of the actions. In ordinary life, ethics refers to the moral standards of societies and can therefore take many forms.

Argued over throughout the centuries and affecting all walks of life, in recent years philosophers have enjoyed vigorous ethical debate over issues such as biomedics, the environment, **gender**, warfare, development and population.

See also Risk society

Ethnicity

A combination of social and cultural characteristics that together form a distinctive social identity.

This is a sociological term that has been used in the last two decades partly to replace the idea of **race** but also to refer, more correctly, to socio-cultural groups that share many common traits. The use of the term 'ethnic groups' carries a difficult connotation because of its use in societies in which a dominant, often white, culture conceives of these groups. These complicated relations between different ethnic groups, a situation now often described as **multiculturalism**, draws partly on the fact that the ethnicity of white groups is somehow invisible and implicitly constructed as superior. Thus ethnicity operates as a signification of inclusion and exclusion, a fact which was very visible when openly racist terms were used but which has now become clouded by the official discourses of **multiculturalism**.

Ethnicity is a wider and more sociological concept than race, which carries with it a sense of biological fixity and **essentialism**. Ethnicity implies belonging to a particular group and has an overtone of active cultural definition rather than biological destiny. The term was originally used in sociology to describe a group identity based on shared religious, cultural or linguistic heritage rather than racial characteristics.

Fundamentally the shift in the use of terms like 'race' and 'ethnicity' mirrors the changing political realities of the postwar world and marks the decline of a white colonial culture which defined itself by the exclusion of other 'inferior' races. This is particularly true in the United States, where the language of race was used to justify segregation and discrimination of quite extraordinary brutality in a nation that laid claim to democracy and equality. Thus the emergence of a **discourse** centred on ethnicity marked the overthrow of a Eurocentric **hegemony** and the opening out of an understanding of cultural and ethnic difference.

In an important 1996 essay, 'New ethnicities', Stuart Hall talked about the way in which a new cultural politics was emerging which 'engages rather than suppresses difference'. By this he means that notions of **identity** and cultural practice are now contested within notions of ethnicity and can be done so in an open multicultural discourse in which ethnicity does not have to claim its place against a hegemonic whiteness.

Ethnography

Direct observation of cultural and social groups by temporarily joining them.

This approach is normally used by anthropologists and involves living with, directly observing and participating in the lives of the study group. Some sociologists adopted the technique in order to facilitate participant observation, although it was always assumed that the observer had no impact on the observed, which is rather contentious these days. Evolving out of the traditional, evolutionary approach to anthropology, contemporary ethnography has also incorporated oral history, participant observation, archival analysis and even group participation in multifaceted research. **Cultural studies** has incorporated many of these approaches in terms of inner-city fieldwork with particular groups and generations.

Existentialism

A philosophy in which 'existence precedes essence'.

This is a term that has both a very general usage—as in existential angst—and a specific philosophical meaning that relates to the existential movement of the postwar era. In its broadest everyday use the term implies the sense of **alienation** and anxiety that besets humankind in modern society, the angst that comes from living in a society that seems to have no meaning. This feeling of isolation and **anomie** is characteristic of much modern literature and loosely describes the random, discontinuous and unpredictable life of humankind in societies where choice is overwhelming.

The specific use of the term is always associated with Jean-Paul Sartre, Simone De Beauvoir and the postwar period in France, but it has its roots in the work of Martin Heidegger and goes as far back as the nineteenth century and Sören Kierkegaard. It is perhaps important to distinguish between the public face of a philosophy—which in this case has become almost a lifestyle—and the historical roots of that philosophy as a mode of thought. Existentialism is fundamentally a philosophy which is concerned with the freedom that humankind has to find its own destiny, an idea very much out of favour at the moment.

De Beauvoir and Sartre were constantly struggling to find a way to express the fact that they were living 'unique' lives for which they were wholly responsible, an attitude that was completely at variance with the dominant strands of Marxism at the time, as well as later structuralist positions. Their central contention was that, since God did not exist, humankind was entirely adrift in a world of meaninglessness and absurdity and therefore decisions about the conduct of one's life were not to be based on **ideology** but on individual choice. This is the existential dilemma which comes before any idea of the essence of life, or the reasoning that might come from authority based on scripture or tradition. Sartre was always looking out for the varieties of 'bad faith' through which he considered people avoided their actual responsibility for themselves, what he termed sinking into 'immanence'.

Fake TV

Television shows that purport to present 'ordinary' people as extraordinary.

The rapid rise of television chat shows that feature 'ordinary' people has been one of the most unexpected phenomena of the last ten years, as has the rise of what are called docu-soaps, which similarly feature ordinary people going about their every-day lives. This new genre of television, in which ordinary people endlessly discuss their emotional and other problems in public, has attracted huge audiences, massive advertising revenue and made stars of presenters like Oprah Winfrey, Jerry Springer and Ricki Lake. Whatever the benefits to the audience of having these personal problems aired on television—in what is fast becoming a kind of electronic intimacy in which the public/private split no longer operates—it is clear that this kind of television appeals to the networks. The economic facts of audience participation shows are fairly obvious: they are extremely cheap to make since there is an endless supply of willing participants who are not, normally, paid. What is even more interesting is the way in which the concept of the personal, and of relationships, is being redefined by television, and by the audience's symbiotic relationship with television.

The pressure on television to produce 'infotainment' or 'edutainment' is relentless and grotesque, and it is here that we enter the world of fake TV. Since television constantly works to deadlines, it is here that the pressure to produce the ordinary as extraordinary shades over into the postmodern. Recent cases in Britain have highlighted the way in which agencies have supplied fake guests to such shows, underlining the fact that much of this television is sensationalised and imaginary, a properly postmodern condition of **hyperreality**. The 'truth' of docu-soaps has begun to be regularly questioned, since the everyday behaviour of the participants is often influenced by the presence of the cameras. In fact what was historically described as 'news-gathering' has begun to take on the same 'constructed-for-television' quality that postmodernists refer to as 'simulation'.

Fake TV is a newly-coined term but it draws attention to the constructed nature of all images, including nature programmes themselves, and to the fact that audiences are both participating in, and understanding, the falsity of television as a medium. Jean Baudrillard famously announced that the Gulf War did not happen, thus both proving postmodernism's grasp of the dominance of Fake TV and announcing its failure to differentiate between fake and reconstruction.

Feedback

A term describing the reception and response of a message.

Many models of communication operate in a one-way flow only, considering just the message and its transmission. Feedback is seen as recognising that communication can be a two-way process, or even form a communication loop. The term comes from cybernetics and refers to the way in which a response can be built into an otherwise linear system. In modern communication and electronic media, the possibility of feedback—or interactivity—is increasingly seen as important. The Internet offers endless possibilities of feedback, of instant response and communication, and it is on this basis that some argue that the Internet is thereby providing new forms of electronic democracy.

In media terms, however, feedback appears to diminish all the time as multinational corporations control the production and flow of programming. In this respect it is interesting to note the recent rise of audience participation programming such as the shows of presenters like Oprah Winfrey, Jerry Springer and Ricki Lake. This is seen as feedback television in that it responds to the audience's demands by elevating the ordinary and the emotional to a public level and is hugely popular. There is an argument that this is fifteen-minute **celebrity culture**, however, and reproduces the sense of a media culture which seeks to constitute the audience in a powerfully symbiotic relationship. It is conceived, then, not as feedback but as circularity.
See also Fake TV.

Feminism

A movement seeking equality for women in a patriarchal society: the theory of equality.

Although a complicated term—indeed some theorists argue that there are 'feminisms' rather than a coherent feminism—there is a general agreement on the specific character of gender relations and the need to reform them. Feminism can be divided historically into three main phases, often referred to as the first, second and third waves. The first phase is usually thought to have begun in the late eighteenth century with the impact of **Enlightenment** ideas of equality, reason and freedom. It was not until the latter part of the nineteenth century that feminism developed into a widespread movement, based around the demand for equal voting rights. This was partly achieved in the early part of the twentieth century but appeared to make little difference to real sexual equality despite the radical and militant campaign waged by the suffragettes in Britain.

The postwar period saw the birth of the second wave of feminism, which was more commonly referred to as the women's movement. It developed in Britain and America, but drew on Simone de Beauvoir's famous 1953 text *The Second Sex* for inspiration. The second wave of feminism began in political struggle of the traditional kind, associated with civil rights and anti-Vietnam war struggles, but rapidly developed into a cultural politics that challenged accepted sex-roles within the wider culture. The slogan of the second wave that reflected this transformation was that the 'personal is political', in itself a radical and far-reaching political strategy. What it meant was that the domain which was traditionally excluded from the political world—personal life—is political in the internal and external sense: internal in that the relations between women and men were relations of **power**—economic, sexual and political power within relationships—and external in the sense that political power (discursive/state power) actually constitutes intersexual relations, the regulation of marriage and the divide between the public and the private. Early feminists (Kate Millett; Juliet Mitchell) argued that power relations are lived subjectively and sexually/psychically; that the crudest experiences of power are played out within reproductive sexuality and familial relations; and that these constitute the foundations of all power relations. Feminist thought expressed itself in new feminist journals, in publishing houses, in consciousness-raising groups and in a critique of traditional male politics with its ideas of leadership and control.

The third wave of feminism can be characterised as the institutionalisation of feminist theory, the impact of feminism on **popular culture** and the critique of phallocentric discourses of sexuality within psychoanalysis and social theory. Emerging only in the 1970s, feminist theory has rapidly developed into a substantive body of thought that has engaged with all of the humanities and has effectively rewritten **psychoanalysis**, literary theory, Marxism and **structuralism**. Questions of **class**, sexuality, the **body**, heterosexuality, **difference** and language have all been foregrounded by feminist theory in order to rethink the basic categories of intellectual **discourse**, and it is in this critique that feminism has had its greatest impact.

See also Post-feminism.

Flâneur

The observer.

This French word means 'stroller', with the particular connotation of 'one who strolls in urban areas'. Baudelaire was the first to use the word in a literary sense, in his descriptions of nineteenth-century Paris. The flâneur (traditionally thought of as male) observes the busy city life around him as he walks the streets, but at the same time he is part of the bustle around him. In other words, he both wants to be seen as well as to see.

The flâneur is a cultural consumer, who experiences life as a series of instantaneous, almost subliminal, impressions. The main question, though, is whether he is a philosopher/voyeur, who considers and decodes the meaning of the life around him, or a shadowy, almost pathetic figure, whose only fulfilment is participating in the transitory nature of other people's lives.

Flow

The movement of time, form and ideas in digital culture.

This is a term that was used initially in discussions of television and was first used by Raymond Williams in the 1970s. It is a feature that fundamentally distinguishes the printed media from the electronic media, of which it is a key structuring principle. Williams was interested in the overall experience of watching television rather than in discrete programmes, and this led him to consider how the flow of images, advertisements, trailers and films constructed a certain kind of viewing experience. In some ways the 'flow' of television resembles what Marshall McLuhan was talking about when he argued that the 'medium is the massage' (McLuhan, 1967), but Williams' use of the term is more sociologically based in the relationship between viewer and medium. The ever-increasing dominance of electronic visual culture in present-day society means that the flow of images and ideas is becoming an important aspect of how that culture is experienced. Film, television and advertisements resemble each other more and more and the visual language they mobilise constructs and reconstructs a particular flow of narrative patterns.

As if to demonstrate the rapidly changing **paradigms** within which **cultural studies** operates, the term 'flow' was taken up by French philosophers Gilles Deleuze and Felix Guattari to refer to a very different cultural approach. Their use of the term draws on psychoanalytic notions of repression and of the way in which society channels and directs libidinal energies, an idea that derives from the **Frankfurt School**'s work on the authoritarian society. Their concern is to liberate the energies they see as being blocked and channelled in particular ways within society by the practices of **psychoanalysis** and the oppressive forms of social organisation that derive from social and psychological control. They argue that psychoanalysis is hierarchical, that it benefits social control, and that only an anarchical, free-flowing politics is sufficient to overcome the dominant system. Like other poststructuralist and postmodern writers, Deleuze and Guattari elaborate an approach which celebrates flow rather than control or rationality, and seeks to delineate multiplicity and **difference** by working through diversity and liberating the flow of ideas and creativity. This approach boils down to a kind of anarcho-spontaneist claim that micro-political activity unsettles dominant **power** relations.

Manuel Castells uses the term to describe the flow of information in electronic communication, a facet of modern life that is increasingly dominant. Financial markets, news services, information networks and the Internet itself are all dependent on the flow of information, and its organisation and distribution. Castells is concerned with the central impact of **globalisation** as the transformation of everyday space and time, and with the ways in which the flow of wealth, people, information, crime, **culture** and technology subvert national boundaries and controlled spaces.

Fordism

The organised mode of mass-production based on assembly-line manufacture.

A system by which a manufacturing process is fragmented into its component tasks and thus easily supervisable by management. First implemented in the Ford Motor factory, it is also known as Taylorism.

Formalism

A theory of form in which form tends to be elevated over control.

Formalism can either be a negative term referring to a tendency to elevate form over content, or a term that refers to a specific Russian school of literary theory. The formalists—known as the Opayez—were a group of theorists, centred around Victor Shlovsky, who came together in the cultural ferment after the Russian Revolution. Despite the political and cultural struggles that went on around them, their approach was entirely focused on the idea that the works of literature were separate from everyday life and based on a different—literary—language. This relatively simple-sounding idea led the formalists to claim that literature 'defamiliarised' everyday life, or made it strange in order to present a different reality.

What also set the formalists apart from much traditional literary criticism was their concern with the techniques of literary style, what it was about literary language that made it so different. They were attempting to develop what they called a 'scientific' analysis of literature, which drew out how it departed from ordinary conventions. This kind of approach led to the elevation of form over content and to the sorts of arguments that are often denounced as formalist. The attempt to isolate what was specific about literary language meant that the social and cultural content of the text was ignored, thereby reducing the meaning of a novel or poem to its mechanisms, and whether they were original, different or strange.

The charge of formalism is, then, found proven on the one hand, but on the other hand the insistence on examining the nature of form proved extremely interesting historically in the development of **structuralism**. Roman Jakobson provides the historical connection between the early formalists, the Prague school and the rise of structuralism in the 1960s. He developed the formalist notion of the difference between 'plot' (*sjuzet*) and 'story' (*fabula*) in his idea of the 'poetic function', or the mode of being of a poem that defines its achievement of literariness. These are ideas that clearly had influence on structuralism and **semiotics**, and writers like Roland Barthes, with his notions of **writerly/readerly** texts.

Frankfurt School

A group of critical Marxist theorists originally based in Frankfurt.

Properly named the Institute for Social Research in Frankfurt, it was formed in 1923 and included, among others, Max Horkheimer, Theodor Adorno, Herbert Marcuse and, sometimes, Walter Benjamin. These theorists were, and still are, important because they were the first to address the question of the importance of the mass media in advanced capitalist societies. They realised that the role of **ideology** in **society**, especially in terms of social control, had been significantly altered by the arrival of mass communications. The conclusions they drew from their analysis of the dominance of the **mass media** were profoundly pessimistic—in fact they saw the mass media as completely dominating consciousness, thus more or less extinguishing the possibility of revolutionary struggle. High culture was seen as the last bastion of criticality against the ever-rising tide of commercialised inanity, and as being under threat by the mass media.

Walter Benjamin developed a more subtle analysis of the potential role of the mass media, projecting certain positive aspects, but the work of the school overall was clearly influenced by their experience of fascism. Their 'critical theory' was a reworking of orthodox Marxism, which they saw as being economically determinist, but they also incorporated **psycho-analysis** and a theory of the 'culture industries'.

The Frankfurt School coined the term 'culture industries' to describe the way in which they saw the press, entertainment and radio industries becoming capitalist institutions based on profit making, audience massification and the commodification of cultural output. They saw artwork as being stripped of its originality, made repetitive through formulas of success, and being aimed at specific markets where the manipulation of audiences as passive consumers was the key aim. They pointed to popular music as being an example of mass-produced, homogeneous commodities which were produced for mass consumption and maximum profit.

Their emphasis on the industrialisation of culture was revolutionary in its time but later came to be seen as both reductionist, in that it failed to understand the changing nature of the marketplace, and pessimistic, in that it failed to recognise that consumers acted not just in passive terms but also in critical and rejectionist ways. Their analysis of the industrialisation of culture and of the changes in the psychology of consumption has remained influential, however, and has been recently rediscovered.

Functionalism/structural functionalism

Sees societies as cohesive social systems where all parts ideally function to maintain social equilibrium.

Functionalists see **society** as the sum of all its parts and consider each part's contribution to the whole. They see the family as a micro-social system designed to provide and socialise new members of society. Structural functionalism dominated American social theory in the 1940s and 1950s and is particularly associated with the work of Talcott Parsons. Elements which disrupt the system are called dysfunctional.

See also Norm.

Gaze

The look: ways of viewing, seeing or visualising reality.

The idea of the gaze—the look, the forms of viewing and thereby controlling, or attempting to control, the world—has been an important idea this century. One of the best general introductions to this field can be found in John Berger's *Ways of Seeing*, a book about how we view art and what this means. The way in which we view the world, the process of how we subject the world to our vision, plays an important role in the construction and maintenance of **power** relations. A doctor looks at—'examines', views a patient and thereby subjects the patient to his/her gaze of objectivity and control. Similarly, the colonialist—'master of all he surveys'—subjects the colonised to his imperial gaze, which constructs them, sees them, as non-subjects, as the inferior objects of his gaze.

This idea was taken up by Michel Foucault, and particularly in film theory. The central idea of the gaze goes back to Sigmund Freud and his theories of scopophilia, the drive to look, to master the world. Jacques Lacan developed these ideas into an important element in his theory of **subjectivity**. Within existentialism another, more reflexive, idea of the gaze gained some prominence, but was criticised by Lacan.

The idea of the gaze has been most important in film studies, particularly in the work associated with the journal *Screen*. The classic statement of this approach in film theory was that of Laura Mulvey in 'Visual pleasure and narrative cinema', in which she argued that the cinematic gaze was inherently masculine (Mulvey, 1975). How Mulvey arrived at this position relates to her use of Freudian, Lacanian and Althusserian theories of inter-pellation and her analysis of the male spectator as identifying with the perfect image on the screen, which clearly relates to fantasy and pleasure. Cultural theory about the film spectator goes back to Walter Benjamin, who rightly pointed out that film was a radical new medium that would affect the viewer in interestingly different ways. He also pointed out that **psycho-analysis** and film were connected in the way that they presented images and dived below the surface to represent other, repressed forces. It is this connection that Mulvey is considering in her development of a theory of the male gaze and its psychoanalytic basis.

First Mulvey considers Freud's notion of scopophilia, which basically means a pleasure in looking, an emotion that is at the basis of all the visual arts but which is heightened in the cinema. Mulvey then links this viewing pleasure to the mirror-phase, Lacan's term for the moment when the baby sees its unified, perfect image in a mirror and assumes a relationship to that perfect image, an imaginary unity that is the self reflected back upon itself. The male gaze in the cinema adopts this viewing position of identifying with the perfect image on the screen in a narcissistic way that both valorises the male viewer and sees women as sexual objects to be looked at. The position of women in cinema is, then, essentially to be looked at as they had always been in art: an object of pleasure. Conventional cinema for Mulvey is masculinised, and its realist conventions reproduce the dominance of patriarchal social relations in providing a structure that accommodates the male gaze.

There have been many criticisms of Mulvey's arguments, mainly centred around the failure of her analysis to allow for a more positive female gaze—like much other Lacanian analysis, it appears to trap the viewer in structures that are irreversible. Mulvey modified her position in later articles as **cultural studies** moving more towards ethnographic notions of spectatorship and less structuralist readings of viewers and subjects. Lesbian and **queer theory** have also strongly criticised the fixed positions adopted by Mulvey and argued for a different economy of the gaze. In an electronic culture that is predominantly visual, however, the gaze—whether male, female, queer, voyeuristic or inattentive—is an area of some theoretical importance. The relationship between surveillance, the gaze and political control is rapidly becoming a central question in cities where all citizens are constantly watched by cameras.

Geek

A postmodern form of sexuality.

This is a very recent term that comes from the new language of the computer era. It refers to someone who is absorbed in the technicalities of computing, and whose whole outlook is bound up with computers or science. It is a derogatory term which suggests being cut-off from ordinary life in exchange for a life lived out through science and technology. It seems to derive from American high school discourse and the distinction between sportsmen (jocks) and those who are academically inclined. However it does have a specificity in relation to new technology because it is possible, through computers and **virtual reality**, to live a physically anti-social life that becomes de-socialised and obsessed with technical detail. Geeks are potentially the prototypes of new men and women in virtual reality. A recent Silicon Valley dating agency has reported that 80 per cent of 20–25-year-old computer workers have requested their services, in itself an interesting transformation of personal relations. Bill Gates is sometimes quoted as the world guru of geeks. The most interesting question, however, is why we need this term at all?

Gender

A contested term that refers to socially defined sexual characteristics.

Where traditional thought about masculinity and femininity was entirely based on biology, **feminism** set out to rethink this divide as socially constructed and thus began to use the term 'gender' to differentiate it from sex. The concept of gender developed its more contemporary usage through the confrontation between second-wave feminism and the prevailing ideologies of naturalism, which explained the social position of women as being fixed by biological nature. Women's liberationists and, following them, feminist scholars, challenged both the **ideology** that women were 'sex objects' defined by their presumed sexual natures as objects of, and circumscribed by, male **desire**; and the perhaps more hegemonic idea that biological natures—maleness and femaleness—were both fixed and unchangeable.

The idea that sexual nature preceded the social and gave shape to it in the form of a myriad of sexual divisions between women and men, home and work, private and public, as well as emotional and intellectual capacities was one which feminists had necessarily to challenge if the appeals for social change in the position of women were to be at all successful. Gender was the concept which was used to begin this challenge: it addressed the historical diversity of definitions of masculinity and femininity as well as the cross-cultural differences measuring the complexity of gender regimes, made visible by the early comparative and interdisciplinary scholarship undertaken by feminists. The concept of gender was deployed to specify analytically the social, cultural, economic and political contours of gender constructions which shaped gender regimes. It mapped a domain for strategic intervention and change which illuminated the historicity of gender identities and the complex relationship between **identity** and **subjectivity**.

Like all pioneering concepts, however, the theory of gender lost much of its innovative force after the sustained scrutiny it was subjected to in the prodigious developments in feminist philosophy and theory. The problems were many: first, the concept of gender did not extend to an explanation of the systematic discrepancies of **power** which attached to masculinity and femininity and which, indeed, had been precisely what early feminists were attempting to overcome. In stressing, moreover, the social nature of gender—that is, of masculinity and femininity—little analytic attention was extended to the parallels between biological difference and gender hierarchies: masculinity tended to be associated with males and femininity with females. The cultural or historical implications of these terms varied but their attachment to specific sexual **difference** did not. Although this did not preclude the possibility of 'reinscripting' these cultural definitions into more egalitarian, progressive and democratic identities, it left unexplored the relationship between biology and gender.

The idea of an essential sexual nature was weakened but not entirely dislodged by the feminist deployment of gender and the competing positions of essentialist and social constructionist ideas of sexual difference became locked into an impossibly polarised debate. This deadlock was finally broken by Diana Fuus, who pointed out that biological **determinism** was itself a social construction with a variety of discursive strings to its bow; and social construction similarly invoked an essential subject. The duality of sex/gender was further challenged by Judith Butler and her concept of gender as performance, the linguistic re-enactment that produces the activity of gendered identity and subjectivity.

Another seam which has been mined in an attempt to resolve the difficulties inspired by gender is the shift to the idea of the **body**. Here too, however, the idea of the sexed body is marked by the seemingly intractable difficulties inspired by using irreducible categories to illuminate social analysis in the service of political objectives for democratic change.

Perhaps the most significant critique of the centrality of gender in feminist theory was mobilised by black feminists who argued that it had acted to displace the other axes of cultural identity, not least that of **race**. As such, gender had functioned to obliterate differences between women, differences which incorporated hierarchies of race, **class** and **ethnicity** and which, more importantly, gave the lie to the claim that femininity implied powerlessness. Gender, in other words, had to be specified in the way in which it was wrought through the complex and changing intersections constituting cultural identities.

Displaced from its privileged position in feminist theory, the lacunae inspired something of a crisis in feminist thought in raising the spectre of a collective which could no longer represent itself as a political constituency: women were different from men but also different from each other, and the promise of gender as a unifying platform for feminist strategic ambitions seemed lost. What was gained, however, was a widespread recognition that gender was a key modality of social analysis, a recognition that measured a considerable distance from the pre-feminist conception of reductive and opportunistic biological determinism.

Genealogy

A radical approach to the analysis of knowledge.

The nineteenth-century German philosopher Friedrich Nietzsche showed that ethics were not God-given but, rather, produced by social and historical processes. Michel Foucault adopted and expanded Nietzsche's theories to encompass all forms of knowledge production. In opposition to the traditional belief of systematic historical progression, genealogy focuses on the complex and contingent aspects of history.

Foucault used genealogical analysis to study three centuries of clinical definitions and treatments of madness, showing how to a great extent insanity is socially and historically, rather than biologically, constructed.

Genotext/Phenotext

The difference between the emotional structures and the signifying patterns of language.

A set of terms used by Julia Kristeva in her analysis of the connection between the functions of language and the formation of the **subject**. Kristeva, as a psychoanalyst, rejects the formalism of much semiotic theory, in which the subject is fixed in and through language, and argues that the subject is always a 'subject-in-process'. That is to say, Kristeva sees language as a dynamic process, not as a static rule-bound system.

The genotext is not the language itself, but rather a process, the underpinnings of language. The phenotext is more like the actual form and language of communication, the literal level at which meaning is constructed. Kristeva argues that genotext and phenotext do not operate in isolation but are always fused in the signifying process. The importance of these terms resides in their use within Kristeva's overall arguments about the social functioning of language, where the unanalysable, the repressed, is seen as being equally as important as the logical structures of the forms in which it is represented. To this end, Kristeva also talked about 'semananalysis'—focusing on both the materiality of language, its sound and rhythm, and the poetics of language, which challenges the simple communicative model of language—as a signifying system.

Globalisation

**The process by which the world becomes increasingly one
market, dominated by electronic culture.**

This is a term that is of very recent origin and belongs to the
world of business as much as to sociology or **cultural studies**.
It refers to the way in which the nation states of the world,
and their economies, have developed into a global market in
which instant communication and permanent trade have utterly
transformed the everyday world. It is difficult to pinpoint when
true globalisation began, but it was probably in the late 1970s
and has increased exponentially in the last ten years with the
Internet and global communications becoming established facts
of world finance and trade. Global, 24-hours-a-day communication and financial markets are the fundamental basis of these
new systems which are redefining our cultures. The creation of
a One World order in which nation states are of secondary
importance is the fundamental characteristic of this new global
system.

Satellite communication is probably an apt metaphor for
this new global order. The first satellite went up about 30 years
ago and now there are more than 200 commerical and military
satellites in operation. New ones are launched so often that
they are only reported in the global media when the launch
fails and several hundred million dollars of new technology goes
up in smoke. Global satellite communication is now instant,
permanent and technologically reliable, which means that war,
World Cup soccer and the Oscars are live global events with
audiences of billions rather than millions.

Whilst the most obvious result of globalisation is instant
communication and global live television, the most powerful
force is undoubtedly global financial markets. The scale of
monetary flow around the world on a daily basis is now so great

and so instantaneous that governments appear to have very little control over the process. It is now commonplace for multinational companies to shift their factories, their production and their wealth to countries that provide the most beneficial financial climate. If governments adopt policies that the 'markets' disapprove of, reaction can be swift and destructive: currencies can collapse overnight and economies be swept into massive recession and unemployment in a matter of weeks. This side of globalisation presents a much less positive picture than the globalisation of **culture**, which undoubtedly has positive effects in increasing intercultural understanding. Which of these faces of globalisation is the most dominant is a major interdisciplinary debate.

Globalisation as an economic force produces a new international division of labour in which capital flows around the world as transnational corporations seek the cheapest labour force, thereby eroding working conditions and trade union rights. Globalisation also affects global agriculture, turning local production-for-consumption communities into cash-crop economies that produce for a global market. The most recent production of genetically modified food, and seed, for the global market ushers in a new phase of global control and transformation of social relations. Genetically modified seed contains a 'terminator' gene that switches off the normal reproductive cycle of plants and ensures repeat sales of the seed. The implications of this global technological control are politically threatening.

At the socioeconomic level, then, globalisation seems to be gathering momentum, but the cultural question seems much more open to debate. Even with the rise of the Internet and global communication, the global village often appears to be more of a media reality than a cultural reality. Globalisation as a world-market system is, however, the dominant reality in analysing the nature of change and development in society today.

Governmentality

Big Brother is watching you.

Michel Foucault devised the term 'governmentality' to describe the increasing tendency over the past two centuries for the **state** to intervene in the lives of its citizens. There have been two main consequences of this change. First, citizens are regulated by the state, its institutions and **discourses**, for example, compulsory education and the census system. Second, citizens are educated to regulate and monitor their own behaviour (self-governance). However, neo-liberal ideas, which are fundamentally anti-state, have eroded this governance.

Grand narrative

All-encompassing theories that dominate western rational thinking.

A grand narrative is really just another name for an all-encompassing theory, one that seeks to explain everything in its own terms. **Enlightenment** theory, or rationality, is seen as one of the grand narratives that we have to put behind us in order to see the world as it now, supposedly, is. This idea came out of the work of Jean-François Lyotard, who argued that all of these grand narratives were historically oppressive and that we have now all seen through them. **Postmodernism** is based in this rejection of grand narratives, claiming that we now occupy a world in which mini-narratives are the way we live our lives. Feminist theory argues that patriarchal society is one of the remaining grand narratives, and sociologists still maintain that **class** and economic power play a dominant role in shaping social reality.

One problem with this idea of grand narratives is whether anyone absolutely believed in them anyway, also whether they were as all-encompassing as the postmodern argument implies. Grand narratives used to be called theories, and renaming them as grand narratives perhaps reflects the mood of the era that we live in. The pluralist position that postmodernism wants to argue sounds a good deal more convincing if we accept that in the 'bad old days' there were all these oppressive grand narratives which limited debate and which postmodernism is here to sweep away. In fact the Renaissance supposedly swept away all the grand narratives of the mediaeval era, and then the Enlightenment swept away all of the irrational doctrines of the post-renaissance, and so on. The obvious, if rather trite, question is whether the theory of mini-narratives is itself actually an all-embracing theory or grand narrative.

Habitus

A system of shared social dispositions and cognitive structures.

This is a term that is associated with the work of Pierre Bourdieu, a French sociologist who has spent a good deal of time and energy attempting to reconstruct theory so that it reflects a practical sense of the complexities of social life and the human agent's place within it. Bourdieu's notion of habitus was developed as an alternative to the dualities of **subjectivity** and **structuralism**, the former reducing social problems to the question of consciousness and the latter simply seeing the individual as the 'bearer' of unconscious structures.

The notion of habitus is similar to the notion of 'ways of life' in that it reflects the concrete experiences that the individual acquires through socialisation, and which remain with them throughout life. Bourdieu describes habitus as being a 'durable, transposable system of definitions' which is initially acquired by the child in the family and which reflects the patterns of

behaviour or the cultural modes, both conscious and unconscious, through which family life is reproduced. Bourdieu, then,
suggests that onto this primary habitus there is subsequently
built a secondary or tertiary habitus as the individual develops
through different social institutions, in particular education.
There is clearly a relationship between the idea of habitus and
Bourdieu's notion of **cultural capital**, although habitus is more
the lived experience of **culture** rather than its social dimension.
Bourdieu argues that early socialisation exerts a defining shape
on the outlook of the individual, and the unconscious structures
of that habitus stay with the individual.

Bourdieu is also interested in the place of tradition and history
in the formation of habitus, an approach that clearly puts him
in opposition to the de-historicising tendencies of **postmodernism**. Bourdieu sees everyday, habitual practices as reflecting
these deeper historical trends in which individual outlook is
moulded by wider, shared patterns of behaviour which are taken
for granted or natural. The usefulness of the idea of habitus is
that it concentrates on the importance of lived experience, on
the everyday, while not losing sight of the fact that wider social
structures are involved.

Anthony Giddens has a similar notion in what he calls practical consciousness, by which he means the day-to-day
experience of lived reality which is rarely reflected upon. The
notion of habitus extends, however, to the structured domains
of social institutions and groups like the army, the church,
politics or artistic life—each has its own habitus. In other
terminology we might talk about the culture of a particular
institution but the idea of habitus is more useful because it
emphasises both the structured nature of institutional life and
also the unconscious dimension of habitual behaviour, something which has a powerful hold on social groups. Bourdieu
(1990) sums this up rather well: 'The habitus-embodied history,
internalized as second nature and so forgotten as history, is the

active presence of the whole past of which it is the product'.

Habitus can be compared to a 'feel for the game', or a practical sense of how to operate in any situation, which draws on the inherited patterns of behaviour that are ingested with the family meal. It is a kind of second sense by which the individual reacts and which betrays that individual's origins.

See also Doxa.

Hegemony

The exercise of cultural and social leadership by a dominant group.

Important in much **cultural studies**, media studies and feminist understanding of cultural dominance, the theory of hegemony is partly aligned to the culturalist approach to historical studies but also to the work of the Birmingham Centre for Cultural Studies. The concept is always associated with Antonio Gramsci, an Italian Marxist who used it to describe the way in which a dominant **class** maintained its position not through force, but through consensus or ideological leadership.

Gramsci was interested in the important question of why dominated classes seemed to give easy consent to the rule of an elite, how their 'hearts and minds' were won over to a system that exploited them. Marx's theory of **ideology** had a mechanistic view of how 'the ruling ideas were those of the ruling class' based on **power** and force, but this approach did not explain the way in which subordinate groups seemed spontaneously to embrace the ideas and culture of the dominant elites. Gramsci was interested in the way that **culture** itself was a site of the management of everyday life and ideas, how the practices and patterns of a lived culture were produced and reproduced. This question of cultural control is now particularly important in a media-dominated world where politics and culture are often the same thing.

Gramsci was imprisoned by the Italian fascists in the 1930s, where he did most of his writing under extremely difficult conditions. This had two results: his work was cryptic to avoid the censor, and it took many years for his work to emerge into the mainstream of European thought. The rise of fascism in Italy, which had a populist basis to it, led Gramsci to question the mechanical model of class solidarity that had been dominant in much Marxist thought and to replace it with a dynamic notion of the function of hegemony. By this Gramsci meant that a class didn't automatically hold political and cultural dominance but had to work at it, constructing hegemonic alliances with other groups and factions. Gramsci did not ignore the fact that political force was used, and he always saw the **state** as the main coercive instrument, but he emphasised the nature of cultural and ideological struggle and traditional Marxism's neglect of that struggle. Gramsci understood the way that, through ideological work, startling images and audacious appeals to common sense could win over the consent of groups to whom the interests of the company, or the state, are actually opposed. There was something fashionable and startling in Mussolini's style and approach to the masses in winning them over to fascism, and it was this that Gramsci understood; hegemony is a curious process which should not be confused with cultural dominance. **Thatcherism** also contained some of these elements.

Hermeneutics

Understanding how understanding works: a theory of interpretation.

This is another term that goes back to the Greeks but which has gained a particular meaning in late twentieth-century **cultural studies** debates, particularly in literary studies. Its basic philosophical meaning refers to translating something not understood—a text—into a comprehensible form. We might say it refers to the process of interpretation, and it was generally used to describe the interpretation of biblical texts. Its current usage refers to our understanding of how understanding takes place, particularly in relation to how readers understand the meaning of works of art and literature.

Historically, hermeneutics related to an activity of deciphering which implied that only a certain group, an elite, understood the messages found in particular texts; often these people were priests who controlled religious functions. The term itself refers back to Hermes, the messenger-God of the Greeks, whose job it was to explain divine thinking to the mortals, and that general sense of hermeneutics as being about the interpretation of something beyond ordinary comprehension has persisted.

It is interesting to note that a number of important historical changes took place around the question of the interpretation of texts, almost always religious texts, and of course the criticism of the Roman Church by Martin Luther involved just such interpretation. The Protestant Reformation saw the development of a radical critique of the Catholic Church's claim to have sole competence in interpreting the Bible, and this led to the creation of a new body of thought and practice which eventually led to modern hermeneutics as we know it. Over the past 300 years, hermeneutics has developed in the German Protestant tradition, culminating in the work of phenomenologist Edmund Husserl, Martin Heidegger and Hans-Georg Gadamer.

In the nineteenth century hermeneutics became a broader philosophical theory of human understanding, concerned with the techniques and procedures of how understanding operated— that is to say, a concern with how texts produce meaning and how readers comprehend it. Literary studies was especially interested in how understanding operated at a particular time, since the question of whether a text had a trans-historical meaning or was limited by historically specific readers was central to theories of how literature worked.

Interpretation as such has become a very significant issue within **poststructuralism**, which postulates both the death of the author and the indecipherability of either meaning or intention in literature. The historically stable basis of interpretation has clearly vanished along with the author and, in the age of **deconstruction**, hermeneutics could be said to be the science of optimism opposed to a pessimism of the intellect.

Hot and cold media

A basic distinction in the work of Marshall McLuhan.

This opposition between different modes of media was central to McLuhan's idiosyncratic discussion of how electronic and other media function, and is more metaphoric than analytic. A hot medium, according to McLuhan, is one which extends a single sense in 'high definition', like radio or television, and which leaves little to be completed or reacted to by the audience. By comparison, a cool medium such as the telephone requires the receiver to complete a lot of the message, so it is a high-participation medium. Like much else of McLuhan's approach, this definition seems to see technology as the determining force in communication, and to collapse the message into the medium.

As electronic technologies converge, this kind of distinction seems to have less and less purchase on communication studies. **Technological determinism** is a powerful current in much discussion of new technologies, however, and Baudrillard's work often seems to have overtones of McLuhan's views of technology's independent influence. The rise of the Internet and computer culture has given further impetus to ideas about media determination, indeed the media is becoming the mythology.

Some of the discussion of **cyberspace** seems to take on the proselytising fervour of McLuhan's more wildly optimistic approaches.

Humanism

A theory that puts the 'human' at the centre of analysis; the 'religion of humanity'.

This is a term which has taken on many different connotations, particularly in the last three decades with the arrival of **structuralism** and its deep anti-humanism. In the most general sense of the term it is used to apply to all currents of thought which place emphasis on humankind rather than on God or nature. This broad definition of humanism goes back to Renaissance thought and that historical era when the object of study was shifting from the divine back to 'classical' culture. The later, nineteenth-century meaning of the term was more closely related to the secular idea of promoting humankind over religious ideas: humanism as a kind of atheism.

At the heart of the philosophical position of humanism is the idea that humans possess capacities, like language, that set them apart from all other species and from nature. It is this philosophical position which is attacked by structuralists, poststructuralists and feminists, who argue in different ways that the idea of the autonomous self, the human individual, is ideological and linked with the idea of human nature, which is ultimately neither natural nor simply human but a product of language and misrecognition. Whether humanist ideals have any currency today remains to be seen; **postmodernism** and **poststructuralism** claim to have almost abolished the individual and notions of humanity, but there is a stubborn flicker of Enlightenment resistance in the traces of rational thought which emerge from the bunkers of **liberalism.**

Hybridity

Seen as a characteristic of postcolonial societies, the combination of different elements.

This term derives from the traditional usage of hybrid, meaning to cross together two different things, especially plants or words, and is used in literary and post-colonial studies to point to the way certain kinds of texts combine different forms and methods. In particular, postmodern texts are seen as hybrid, combining different forms and styles and undermining traditional ideas of the text as a unified **discourse**. Postmodern texts have a shifting, ironic and playful character, seeking to subvert the boundaries between old-fashioned distinctions like 'high culture' and 'low culture'. Post-colonial texts contain the kind of hybrid fusion of cultures which shows how an ambivalent space is created through the interaction of elements that are reordered, re-worked, in an anti-hegemonic mode.

Hybridity, according to Homi K. Bhabha, is a key concept in post-colonial studies because it allows **culture** to be thought of as the interaction between different forms and discourses rather than as the conflict or **binary opposition** of superior/inferior cultures. Hybrid culture—and possibly hybrid subjects—reflects the present-day realities of shifting and interpenetrating cultures. Hybridity gives rise to a notion of a space that is 'in-between' dominant cultures, 'the cutting edge of translation and negotiation'.

Hybridity is also sometimes used as a term to reflect the mixing of genres and approaches in art, like collage or **brico-lage**, and identities can be seen as hybrid.

Critics of the notion suggest that it is too loose an idea and does not deal with gendered identities, or the specificities of **class**, caste and **race** but merely generalises about global cultures.

Hyperreality

A postmodern term that conceptualises the altered nature of reality that is characteristic of this phase.

The hyperreal is understood as being a simulation of the real, a reconstruction of the ordinary as larger than life media representations that become the real or, more properly, the hyperreal. This is a very recent concept that comes out of the work of Jean Baudrillard and Umberto Eco and is central to the arguments about the nature of the postmodern world.

Baudrillard argues, in a reversal of Walter Benjamin's discussion about the **aura** of the **authentic** object, that the imitation of the original is now preferred to the real, the copy becoming more real than the real. Put at its crudest, which sometimes seems pertinent, Baudrillard appears to argue that Disneyland becomes more real than the 'ordinary real'. This produces a society of the **image**, in which media domination saturates the horizon with endless images that obliterate the real.

It is a concept entirely of the media age, and one which essentially accepts the media world as the ideological horizon of all spectators. The argument that history has been replaced by hyperreality is perhaps inflected by looking at the fact that Disneyland in Paris nearly closed down through lack of spectators, entertainment not always being a sufficient simulation of escape to make reality avoidance profitable.

Icon/iconic

A sign that resembles its referent, an image that is emblematically important.

This is a term that derives from the work of the American thinker Charles Pierce, a philosopher who apparently first translated the term 'semiotic' from the Greek, thereby originating what French thinkers have continuously claimed as their own. His work is now more recognised in **semiotics**, particularly his three definitions of the **sign**: icon/iconic, index and **symbol**.

Icon/iconic describes a sign which in some way resembles the object it represents, for example, the word 'bang' sounds like the thing it describes. Unlike the 'arbitrary' signs that Ferdinand de Saussure discussed, iconic signs appear to have some relationship to the object, or referent, that they designate. In semiotic terms, this kind of sign is known as motivated, which means that the meaning relationship is partially constructed through the obvious relationship of the sign to the signified. A painting of a Madonna is iconic, just as a photograph of a haystack is, but a sign is never fully iconic, even though it may have this relationship of similarity. The importance of this idea is that it draws attention to the way that signs function in language, and shows that there may be a relationship to the thing represented. Indexical signs, on the other hand, have a connection—such as smoke to fire, or rain to clouds—whereas symbols are seen in the same way that Saussure viewed signs, as arbitrary.

Perhaps the more powerful use of the term is the one that derives from religion, from the idea of sainthood, and which spills over into **popular culture** in describing someone who is a star, a **celebrity**. Princess Diana was regularly referred to as an icon of our age, along with the rather aptly named Madonna, Mother Theresa, Michael Jordan, and many others of similar celebrity status. To be an icon is, interestingly, slightly different to being a mere celebrity—the distance between the public and the star is of a qualitatively different nature. An iconic figure, like Marilyn Monroe or Che Guevara, is deeply representative of fantasies of otherness, of beauty, of unobtainability, of extra-terrestriality—in other words, of religious projection. Our culture, stripped of traditional religious feelings, takes refuge in idolising celebrity figures in order to create patterns of symbolisation. The manipulation of such a culture is the basis of advertising and entertainment, which together create a particular media culture which is itself iconic.

Identity

The critique of the self-sustaining subject.

According to Stuart Hall (1996b), the question of 'identity' is being vigorously debated in social theory, and these debates ensure that the notion of identity is very much a megaword of current **cultural studies**. Traditionally, identity comes from many sources: from **gender**, sexuality, **class**, **ethnicity**, nationality and cultural industries; it is rarely a straightforward category. The question of identity, who we are, increases in importance as settled identities become fragmented by the powers of social, economic and cultural change. Identity is a location, a place in the discourses of the social construction of being in postmodern society, and is increasingly seen as an important concept in academic discourses. Identity, then, is how we define the **self**, our self, as opposed to others within the possible range of culturally constructed selves.

Traditional cultural studies, and philosophy, assumed a stable, coherent self based in class and gender, and it is that idea which is under attack in much of the current debate. There is, it is claimed, a 'crisis of identity' in the sense that rapidly changing cultural times mean that old-established, settled identities are confronted by doubt and uncertainty and no longer work. The question of identity as a problem for cultural studies arises precisely because no one is certain any longer of what a fixed identity is, and whether it would be a good thing anyway.

Identity—'being the same as'—also implies its opposite— **difference**, being different from something—so we have to ask how this operates.

At one level understanding the construction of identity in present-day society means understanding the whole complex social fabric through which identities are constructed, and the way they respond to the culture through which they are defined. This is why the concept of identity has come into play: it pinpoints a diverse range of meanings about how we live in contemporary society, about ways of life that are changing rapidly.

The questions considered central to thinking about identity can be summarised as: why is identity important today, both individually and collectively? Is there a 'crisis of identity' and what does that mean? Do we need theories of identity, in particular, do we need to conceptualise what identity is? Why does identity always seem to involve an essentialist idea, such as Englishness or Americanness, something that is seen as naturally, essentially just existing? Why are history, **nature** and **culture** all seen as givens, as uncomplicated narratives that give credence to a particular identity? How are the differences between identities marked out and defined? Why do people put so much energy—psychological and social—into maintaining their identities?

Identity as a cultural studies problem revolves around the relationship between identity and **subjectivity**, between defining identity and **other**, or inter-subjectivity, and in defining wider identity or group identity in terms of social and political solidarity. Cultural studies has had to develop a whole new vocabulary to accommodate the fact that contemporary identities are changing and mutating at a pace that has never been witnessed previously. Sexual, cultural and ethnic identities are being rewritten through a cultural politics which makes the political personal and which signifies change and uncertainty as positive characteristics. National identity is becoming globally redundant. The figure of the twenty-first century may be the **cyborg**, and the notion of settled identity may begin to seem like the nineteenth-century novel did to the twentieth century: a historical relic describing an era of settled illusion.

Identity politics

A form of politics based on personal identity rather than class or gender.

This term refers to a form of politics which derived from the political radicalism of the 1960s and which grew, during the 1980s, to become the dominant mode of political organisation, replacing **class** and **state** political struggles with struggles based around **identity**. From the slogan 'the personal is political' developed a politics that expressed the particularities of personal, rather than class, oppression. Groups which had previously felt marginalised began to organise political entities which identified themselves as **black**, as gay, as women, as expressing their shared identity as people. If people had an identity they had a politics was the political reasoning of the time, and this certainly pointed a way out of the fragmenting class- and state-based politics of the postwar era.

The obvious problem in this 'naming and claiming' was that political analyses could be substituted by a basic **essentialism** in which the articulation of an experience gave it legitimacy but failed to point beyond a group self-interest. There has been an argument that a 'strategic essentialism' is sometimes necessary to allow the possibility of minority politics, and this survivalist 'speaking for itself' clearly is sometimes strategically necessary, as are political alliances and theoretical strategies.

Ideology

A term that describes sets of ideas and examines how they can misrepresent the world.

This is an important term that has been hotly contested since it was first used about two centuries ago. It generally means a set of ideas or a body of doctrine that attempts to provide a coherent expression of the world view of a **class**, a social movement or an institution. Exactly how to define ideology has occupied many theorists, particularly within Marxism, sociology and **cultural studies**. At least five main usages of the term can be identified historically, although within recent feminist and postmodern debate it is falling out of use.

Destutt de Tracy first introduced the term around the time of the French **Enlightenment** as a label for his proposed new 'science of ideas'. The historical importance of the concept is that it opened up a way of thinking about the relationship of ideas to their social context, in itself a quite revolutionary move. It is a feature of the Enlightenment that ideas, religions and theories are seen as being man-made rather than divinely given, and this revolution in thinking is held to have inaugurated the modern era.

It was in reaction to the radical ideas of the Enlightenment that French dictator Napoleon Bonaparte used the notion of ideology to launch a conservative attack on radical ideas which were seen to be ideological, that is, based in radical social theory which advocates social change. He talked about the 'doctrine of the ideologues' and how dangerous they were, and this sense of ideology as the guiding ideas of fanatical groups has persisted into the twentieth century, when the 'ideology of communism' was a frequently used phrase. An ideology in this usage is a false set of ideas that leads people astray.

It was in the work of Karl Marx and Friedrich Engels that ideology first came to play an important role in sociological thinking. They argued that ideology was an inevitable part of capitalist society, and that only by penetrating ideology could a rational and scientific understanding of **society** take place. The central idea they advanced was that ideas were socially determined rather than just occurring by some sort of magical process. By this they meant that ideas about people's roles in society came out of the way **culture** and education were organised by a dominant group in society. They also said that the ruling ideas of an epoch were not necessarily the best or the most natural explanations of reality, but simply the ideas of the ruling group and an expression of the ways in which the economic relationships of society were organised to further the interests of that group. The 'dominant ideology' thesis, as it came to be known, has been extremely influential in all areas of social thought, posing a relationship between the way a society is organised and the way that ideologies function within that society.

Marx claimed that ideology is an inevitable part of society's functioning and that it is 'false consciousness' or an illusory representation of the real relations which occur in a society that is hierarchical and based in notions of property and ownership. Ideology is opposed to a scientific understanding of how society functions, and Marx claimed that the science of Marxism would lead to the end of ideology and the establishment of communism. This has proved to be a rather simplified view of the world and has led to the discrediting of Marx's notion of ideology as simply 'false consciousness'.

Marx also used the term in a more neutral sense, however, when he talked about the way in which men struggle over the nature of ideas in terms of philosophy, the law, politics and religion, or culture as a whole. This other use of the concept of ideology refers to the way in which different interpretations of reality compete, with some being given greater attention than others, perhaps because they fit a particular period or social situation.

The rise of structuralist Marxism, particularly in the work of Louis Althusser, led to a great deal of debate about ideology in the mass media. For Althusser (1970), ideology represented an 'imaginary relation to the real', which is to say that it was a form of false consciousness, but not at all a simple illusion. Althusser argued that the forms of socialisation, what he called the interpellation of individuals, produced a situation in which ideology was the linguistic fog in which they 'misrecognised' themselves as free beings. The hidden structures of language and society pinned the individual into accepting **bourgeois** society and their place in it. This was a stronger definition of ideology than that of Marx since it suggested that there was no way out of ideology or oppression (other than scientific Marxism).

The most significant area of debate about ideology in recent history has centred on the mass media and its role in creating ideological forms in society, based on Althusser's work in particular. He argued that the mass media were 'ideological apparatuses' which were centrally concerned with upholding bourgeois society and the dominant ideologies. The work of media studies was to analyse the way that ideology created positions for the viewer/reader to identify with. These ideas were very influential for a while but were severely challenged by **feminism** and **poststructuralism**, which pointed out that **subjectivity** was more fluid, more complex and less determined than the structuralists thought. This was the beginning of the end for the notion of ideology, which began to seem like a kind of **grand narrative** of thinking about individuals in society, and one which failed to reflect the increasing diversity and complexity of **postmodernism**.

Image

A jargon term of advertising and public relations.

For over 400 years the term image generally referred to an actual physical entity such as a painting. With global access to visual and textual media, the term has come to signify more of its original meaning of vision, fantasy or dream (*imago*).

The most common use of the term at the beginning of the twenty-first century is as an abstract concept which can be manipulated as desired. The increasing **globalisation** of communications means that image has become crucial in both public and private spheres. On a professional level, market competition has forced individuals and organisations to pay much more attention to how they are perceived. Hence the growth of the public relations industry in the late twentieth century. Good PR can tailor an image to meet the perceived needs of the electorate for any politician.

On a personal level image is prescribed by dominant cultural **norms**. This places a great deal of moral responsibility on the shoulders of those who control the electronic media. Adolescents are increasingly at risk of psychological disorders from the continual bombardment of unrealistic physical ideals portrayed in the media.

Imperialism

Cultural and economic dominance of one country by another.

Imperialism is a truly ancient cultural practice which reached its peak in the early twentieth century as rival European powers squabbled over the riches of the undeveloped world. The first systematic critique of imperialism by J.A. Hobson treated it as a purely economic concept and it is only in the late twentieth century that the extent of cultural damage caused by imperialism has become apparent. Cultural imperialism is a term that is now used mainly in media studies.
See also Colonialism.

Indigeneity

The relationship between the aboriginal peoples and their traditional tribal lands has become increasingly politicised in many countries around the world. Generally perceived as 'natural', this

relationship is the basis of tension between the original inhabitants of the land and later arrivals.
See also Colonialism, Race.

Information age/Information revolution

The 'e'xplosion.

Seen as the successor to the industrial revolution of the nineteenth century, the information revolution is a grab bag term referring to society's increasing dependence upon electronic transmission of data. Also called the 'information age', it has spawned a new and rapidly changing language of bits and bytes as well as a more conventional vocabulary.

Wealth can now be seen in terms of information rather than money: you can be information rich or information poor. If you wanted to make some conventional money you could set up your own dot.com (Website) and speculate in ecommerce. Hardly anyone uses snail mail any more, rather it's all email zooming along the information superhighway. There's still junk mail, but now it's called spam.

Virtually anything can now be virtual, from war games to sex. However the fact that you're reading this book shows that there's still some way to go before we move entirely online.
See also Cyberspace, Geek, Virtual reality.

Intellectuals

Self-appointed custodians of the tradition of creative thinking of their society.

In its most general sense 'intellectual' was a term that came into being in the nineteenth century and its use at that time marks the beginning of the specialisation of intellectual activity. In its most current use it refers to writers/thinkers who work in the education/ knowledge industries, and who have a particular status.

Transformations of the intellectual field during the twentieth century have brought the role of the intellectual into question, and it was Antonio Gramsci who first theorised these changes. Rather than referring simply to the intellectual elite, the writers and philosophers of a **society**, Gramsci broadens the discussion to include all those involved in intellectual work, such as teachers, journalists and broadcasters. The idea of the intellectual as thinker, what Gramsci refers to as 'traditional intellectuals', is a historically specific role and one implicitly connected with the **culture** and **hegemony** of the traditional ruling classes. These intellectuals are not merely functionaries of the dominant class, but play a particular role as members of the dominant culture. Gramsci also argues that all new social groups must develop their own intellectuals and counter-hegemonic cultural patterns, and challenge cultural dominance at every level of civil society. Gramsci refers to these new intellectuals as 'organic intellectuals', or those whose cultural role is explicitly connected with a particular strata or **class**.

Like the idea of an **author**, the idea of an intellectual has shifted in different historical eras, and the postwar and postmodern eras have seen interesting developments in the social role of the intellectual. During the 1950s, many intellectuals were caught up in opposition to the Cold War, and they most clearly represent the idea of the committed intellectual which emerged from **existentialism** and Marxism. Raymond Williams discusses these intellectuals in terms of their relationships to dominant, residual and emergent groups in society.

Most recently, Michel Foucault has considered the role of the intellectual in a changed societal mode, arguing that the increased complexity of society and its 'regimes of knowledge' puts intellectuals in a position where they can merely expose what he calls the 'politics of truth'. Because of Foucault's arguments about the nature of **power** in society—for him it is dispersed and deployed across the discourses of power and **knowledge**—he does not claim that the intellectual can in any way be representative or organic. He simply states that the intellectual must work with others in particular, local, institutional struggles related to his/her presence as a 'specific' intellectual.

Interdisciplinarity

Studies which draw upon more than one discipline.

The idea of discrete disciplines in the humanities has been under fairly constant criticism since the 1960s, with varying degrees of success. Interdisciplinarity is often quoted as being an aim of intellectual work but simultaneously is looked down upon as not being intellectually rigorous, or desirable. The way that higher education is organised and delivered very much depends on traditional notions of the disciplines—history, literature, geography, media studies, psychology, etc.—but these disciplines are breaking down in a postmodern world in which interdisciplinarity is assumed as part of the modern curriculum. It is an interesting fact of academic life that the organisational demands of an institution seem to dictate the way that a subject is thought about or, in other words, the organisation takes precedence over theoretical boundaries. True interdisciplinarity would do away with the artificial boundaries that are set up in academia.

A good example of the falsity of discrete disciplines is the challenge posed by feminism to traditional subjects. By asking different questions about how **society** works, **feminism** implicitly goes beyond the boundaries of traditional disciplines. Feminism creates another field of inquiry by demanding a different theoretical and methodological framework, one which works in an interdisciplinary mode. The structure of disciplines and the kinds of questions that are asked within a discipline constitute a theoretical field in themselves, one that Michel Foucault particularly addressed and subverted in looking at the history of the development of disciplines or discourses.

The history of literature as a discipline is a good example of how a historical practice develops and operates within certain rules which reinforce both the discipline and its place or function in society at large. In English literature the idea of the civilising force of literature and of transmitting ideas about national **identity** and proper moral behaviour formed the organic core of a discipline which was built up in universities and through literary criticism. The discipline had a role to play in constituting the national **discourse** and in creating the national language, as well as defining a **canon** of 'great' literature. Only through the rise of an inter-disciplinary study of literature—what came to be called **cultural studies**—was the status of literature as such made apparent and its historical functioning unravelled.

Interpellation

The way in which ideology hails and orders subjects.

This is a term used by Louis Althusser (1970) to describe the way in which he saw **ideology** operating in **society**. Under the influence of structuralist theories of language and the thinking of Jacques Lacan, Althusser conceived of ideology as operating like a mechanised system of public loudspeakers that hailed the subject to behave in the prescribed manner. The **subject** recognises him/herself in this being hailed and comes to live in 'imaginary relation to the real'. Althusser is grappling with a dual problem here, that ideology does seem to exercise an iron grip on individuals and yet the way it is lived is indeed the 'real', as well as being illusionary.

This concept was highly influential for a time in the 1970s, particularly in film and **cultural studies**, but came under sustained attack for its ultimately simplistic notion of how individual subjects were constructed through what Althusser called 'ideological state apparatuses'. The difficult question became that of how, if all individuals were interpellated, could any cultural or ideological struggle continue. Feminists, and others, questioned this sense of inevitability about ideological conditioning and, through poststructuralist critiques of fixity and positioning, reintroduced the idea of **agency** and the subject.

Interpretive communities

Groups who communally construct the meanings of texts.

This is a term which has come into use within literary criticism as part of the shift away from historical notions of the text and the author. It is part of a whole approach known as reader-response theory. These interpretive communities are socially constituted groups of readers who, through a kind of collective development, produce particular readings of texts. The approach reverses the traditional idea that the meaning of a work, particularly a literary text, is to be found through a close reading of the text itself. It is mostly associated with the work of Stanley Fish, whose development of reader-response literary theory has been an interesting reaction to structuralist constructions of literary meaning as being located in the forms of the text.

Fish's arguments about the way in which a like-minded group or community shares certain ideas about literary, and other, texts clearly suggest that the production of meaning is located in the interaction of readers rather than in the text itself. For Fish, the reading strategies that a group develops and confirms fix the meaning of a particular text and, since these communities of readers are assumed to be 'informed readers', these socially constructed meanings become dominant. Readers are guided, according to Fish, by 'interpretive strategies' or communally created agreements about attitudes and assumptions which shape how a text is received.

This approach certainly swings the pendulum away from structuralist and deconstructionist theoretical approaches which are entirely text-based, but one may wonder if the elevation of the reader to the status of group **author** may not be a case of collectivity gone too far. Some feminist literary criticism has made interesting use of these ideas, looking at the different ways in which men and women read and produce texts, but even here the question of just how homogeneous the group really is keeps arising. The obvious problem with the approach is that of how, and why, such interpretive communities are formed and whether, in fact, they change and fracture into smaller groups which may disagree about particular texts.

Inter-textuality

The relation between any text and those which precede it.

This is a term that probably derives from Julia Kristeva's use of it, but it is a common poststructuralist idea that refers to the way in which texts are seen as interacting with other texts. The term describes the interdependence of texts, their necessary interrelationship, rather than accentuating their originality or uniqueness. Perhaps it is easier to distinguish between influences, quotations and inter-textuality. When one writer influences another, there is a similarity in style, ideas, presentation or even themes. When a writer overtly quotes from another, whether through imitation, parody or travesty, there is a kind of inter-textuality.

Roland Barthes and Kristeva seem to go even further than this, suggesting that there is an inter-textual system in which texts operate through a kind of unspoken tissue of past citations. Since language is always seen as prior to the acts of reading and writing, it prefigures the **author** and creates a space in which the text operates in relation to all other already existing texts. These radical poststructuralist views see the world as text and all texts as being areas where language and ideas are produced through textual interplay. This kind of inter-textual strategy opens up a space in which canonical texts can be reconsidered in the light of changing textual relations. Inter-textuality, rather like **virtual reality**, is also sometimes seen as the space between texts in which the relationships reconstitute another dimension.

Irony

A form of wit much loved by the British.

Irony is difficult to define precisely, but it has a lot to do with a subtle linguistic exaggeration of certain traits or characteristics. Irony has been called the subtlest comic form and can use either under- or over-statement (hyperbole) to get a laugh. However it must not be confused with sarcasm or satire as irony is a gentle form of humour.

The current trend of **postmodernism** is characterised by an ironic detachment from reality. Umberto Eco has described postmodernism as an attitude in which we cannot get rid of our dearest hopes and beliefs while at the same time we can't support them in public. Irony can also be seen as a lack of engagement with the 'real', or the dominant mode of electronic culture.

Jouissance

A term which describes particular kinds of pleasure, both textual and sexual.

This term means 'pleasure', but it has also acquired a complicated sexual and linguistic connotation in the hands of Jacques Lacan, Julia Kristeva and Roland Barthes. It is, ironically, a term found in Old English but its more recent French meaning is predominant. The use of the term in English draws attention to the fact that pleasure is a little-used term in the English vocabulary; jouissance, with its overtones of sexual pleasure and orgasm, is clearly a foreign notion within the somewhat puritanical outlook of the Anglo-American tradition. It may be one of the defining terms which demonstrate how importing a foreign concept conveys a certain theoretical glamour to what is fundamentally a somewhat confused approach.

French feminists have used the term in a more radical sense to talk about a particular kind of feminine sexual pleasure which they see as being highly disruptive of the dominant symbolic order. Rather than suffering from lack (of the phallus) women, it is argued, experience jouissance or a sexual satisfaction which is unique to women, and outside symbolisation or intelligibility. This idea of jouissance, while appealing, clearly carries an essentialist overtone described in **écriture feminine** as the idea of a pure feminine sexuality. Kristeva celebrates jouissance as being a return to the pre-Oedipal, to the emotive world of being which is expressed in poetry and art, a rather different theorisation. For Lacan, the term is something to do with pleasure, but also with the imaginary unity that the **subject** always seeks but can never regain. For others, jouissance is the pleasure of the text, the hidden sexuality of reading, or the 'sense of ownership', or an unsettling experience. Perhaps the idea of jouissance as an excess, as too much of a theoretical possibility, is the most appropriate method of rendering it as playfulness.

Knowledge

The most useful commodity after money.

Knowledge is generally taken to be a set of ideas or facts that positively describe the world, or some part of it, with the implication that true knowledge is impartial and unbiased, or universal. A good deal of philosophy is concerned with the question of how we know that something is knowledge rather than belief, or how we can have knowledge of the world. Those who claim that the world is directly knowable are called empiricists, but they also tend to believe in the existence of pure scientific knowledge and of 'facts'.

Many twentieth-century philosophers, feminists and postmodernists have criticised the **canon** of empirical knowledge, pointing out the connections between **power** and 'knowledge' as demonstrated in particular viewpoints. By doing this they have adopted a relativist position which can be problematic because it suggests that some forms of knowledge are more valuable than others.

See also Archaeology, Power.

Liberal/ism

A focus on the rights of the individual in society.

Liberalism is a political philosophy which has undergone many changes since its birth in the Renaissance. That said, it is still very influential in democratic societies. Liberalism values the rights of the individual over the demands of a class or caste. Traditional liberalism defends freedom of speech, democratic elections and freedom of religion. It also is tolerant of minorities, at least to some extent. The idea of individual rights is a powerful mythology in the West.

At the turn of the millennium traditional liberalism has been largely overtaken by what is now called **neo-liberalism** or conservatism. This form of liberalism collapses individual rights into market-forces and elevates capitalism as the supreme liberalism.

Logocentrism

The illusion of a guaranteeing presence or centred meaning.

This is a term coined by Jacques Derrida in order to refer to everything in western culture that puts *logos* (or sense) at the centre of its modes of thinking. Like other concepts pressed into service by Derrida, it is an idea without much of a history. It defines, we are told, all systems of thought which depend on what Derrida calls the 'metaphysics of presence', which means that they depend on a non-linguistic presence or centre, like God or the author, to validate linguistic meaning. The whole of human history has apparently laboured under this illusion of the stability of meaning but fortunately Derrida appeared among us in 1966 to show that all language, logic, meaning and writing is merely deferred so that there is nothing left but **deconstruction**. It slightly begs the historical question of all those philosophers who were endlessly concerned with how meaning came about, if one didn't accept the logocentric position, which many of them didn't. The further question is who guarantees the truth of Derrida's position on logocentrism, or the fact that he exists at all, or that he is worth listening to? Or that writing about him means anything?

Marginality/marginalisation

An interdisciplinary term that refers to the way in which certain ideas are made peripheral through exclusion.

This is a term that refers to the ways in which cultures, disciplines and discourses exclude and repress certain groups and terms in the construction of dominant and hegemonic patterns. Through the exercise of **power**, a centre and a margin is created and sustained and certain terms are privileged, an idea that is central to **deconstruction**. The 1960s term **counterculture** demonstrates how powerful the terms of the accepted cultural landscape can be—even the idea of a marginal, non-mainstream culture had had to be reinvented.

The 'marginal' and the 'marginalia' also apply to textual meanings and dominant readings; it was Pierre Machery, a French literary critic, who most strongly argued in the 1960s and 1970s that attention should be paid to the suppressed and marginal spaces of the text, its silences and evasions. Sociology broadened this kind of approach to consider oppressed and marginal groups and intellectuals in society, which constituted an expanded vision of how it was possible to think about the social. Clearly **feminism** opened up these positions as well, since women were distinctly marginalised by a range of practices and discourses in which they were located as inferior.

Mass media

The electronic and print media which, particularly in the case of television, entirely dominate the symbolic economy of the advanced capitalist countries, and are redefining leisure, culture and the nature of inter-personal relations.

Many theorists argue that this is the defining term of the twentieth century. The terms 'mass media' and 'mass culture' are used within the same theoretical framework and refer to the means of mass communication and to the **culture** it produces. It was not until the late nineteenth and early twentieth centuries that literacy was a widespread reality, thus enabling true mass communications. The rise of the mass circulation newspaper in the nineteenth century was the real beginning of an effective mass media, where very large numbers of readers could be part of a simultaneous audience, but it was only with the arrival of radio that this trend became an actuality. Mass communications are

an integral part of the process of industrialisation and moder-
nisation that has transformed capitalist societies during the last
two centuries, and in its most recent phase—that of the **globalisation** of culture—it has assumed a pivotal role in defining
social experience. The media are so widespread and dominant
that it is difficult to encompass them entirely, but they do have
some shared features:

- They speak to widespread, fragmented and extremely large
  audiences simultaneously, usually from a central point.
- The technologies upon which they rely themselves impact
  upon the modes of communication adopted, particularly in
  the way that they centralise the dissemination of information.
- Mass communication is public, and therefore creates a
  particular public space which had not previously existed.
  Traditional face-to-face culture is increasingly replaced by
  anonymous, top-down cultural forms in which the consumer
  is isolated.
- The nature of the relationship between cultural producers
  and consumers, like a writer or playwright and their audience, is also transformed, often into a relationship which is
  implied but not immediate.
- Mass communications facilitate mass propaganda and
  thereby a transformation of the political, as well as the cultural, sphere.
- Mass communications are seen in many theoretical models
  as manipulating the audience, as proliferating the ideologies
  of either the dominant classes or of capitalism.

The two main models of mass communications are state-
controlled mass media, as routinely found in the communist
countries in the twentieth century, or commercially owned and
controlled mass media, the dominant American model. There
has also been the public sector broadcasting model, most

notably the BBC in the UK and the ABC in Australia. These semi-independent institutions, which were meant to serve the 'public interest', have come under strong commercial pressure over the last decade.

The main theoretical approaches to understanding the mass media are communication studies, the sociology of the mass media and semiotic/structuralist approaches. Communication studies tends to consider communication in isolation, looking at the process rather than the institutions, whereas the sociology of the mass media tends to consider the media within socioeconomic functioning as a whole. The most recent strand, that of **semiotics/ structuralism**, tends to consider the way in which meaning is constructed in media outputs and the way in which messages are encoded/decoded. The continuing importance of the analysis of the mass media is demonstrated by the fact that **postmodernism** as a theory is fundamentally based on the assumption, particularly argued by Jean Baudrillard, that the electronic media so dominate society that the only reality is **hyperreality**. In other words reality itself has been displaced by the dominance of the communications industries and their endless production of images and ideas. That the global media dominate culture in present-day societies is almost irrefutable, but whether they have expunged any other reality is a much more debatable question.

Materialism

Once a philosophical theory, now a model of consumerism.

At the turn of the millennium, materialism now has the popular meaning of 'conspicuous consumption'. In sociological terms, it can mean either the cultural value placed on accumulating material possessions or a belief that human life is shaped by the production of goods and services as well as genetic reproduction.

Materialists consider that social systems are determined by material needs and that **nature** has become fully commodified. They would argue that religious prohibitions on food may be the result of adaptation to physical conditions, for example, climate or disease. Anthropologist Marvin Harris argues that cows became sacred to Hindus simply as an adaptation to the need to maintain breeding stock through long droughts. Materialism is also a theory that what exists, exists in space and time.

Mediascape

A term used to describe a particular kind of reality.

This is a term used by Arjun Appadurai in talking about the global cultural economy and the way in which different elements and features of that global culture can be interwoven to form an individual's mediascape. In a postmodern eclectic fashion, some patterns and fragments from global scripts are picked up and worked into an image-based narrative fantasy of social being, the imaginary global citizen living the global consuming lifestyle. These kinds of mediascapes often lead to a sense of dissatisfaction with the constraints of everyday reality.

Message

The content of communication.

A general term in cultural and media studies, made famous by Marshall McLuhan but more often used in a linguistic sense in present-day media/cultural studies. It is argued that the act of communication sometimes needs to be separated from the message itself, or what that act of communication, is about. The message can only be understood within the context of any given act of communication but the process of communication can be studied separately. The importance of this idea of the message is to recognise that all **communication** depends on a sender and receiver, and an act of transmission. As messages pass from the sender to the receiver there are endless possibilities of misunderstanding and interference, which is why the process of transmission needs to be considered separately to the actual message. Messages are also encoded/decoded by senders/receivers and those processes also have to be analysed to understand how messages are communicated.

Marshall McLuhan's particular use of the term was idiosyncratic but highly influential. His famous declaration that the 'medium is the massage' referred to the then new electronic media and to the impact they were having on communications and culture generally. In essence, McLuhan was arguing that the new media, particularly television, so changed the way that information was delivered that they became the message itself. This was a radical idea, drawn in part from Walter Benjamin's earlier analysis of new technology and its impact on traditional culture—what Benjamin had called the era of 'mass reproduction'. Basically McLuhan argued the position that television demanded a new mode of attending to its message, thereby involving a new mode of participation, of reacting, of being. This argument has repeatedly been criticised for **technological determinism**, reducing the message to the technology and the means of communication, but it has had considerable impact in **cultural studies**, particularly in its revived form in the postmodern approaches of Jean Baudrillard.

Metanarrative

Stories about stories (Jean-François Lyotard).

This term is used to describe any theory which claims to provide a universal explanation. The classic example is Marxism, which

was heavily criticised by Lyotard as authoritarian and restrictive of individual creativity. Perhaps an overused concept.
See also Grand narrative.

Metaphor/metonymy

**Metaphor: the substitution of one term for another.
Metonymy: the substitution of an element of a term for the term itself.**

Roman Jakobson (1956) was the first to posit a distinction between the two terms. At the time, he was studying two forms of aphasia, a condition in which the brain's cognitive and language abilities are damaged or 'rearranged' following an injury. The first took the form of a deficiency in selection or substitution of an appropriate word; the second, a deficiency in combining or contextualising words.

Jakobson applied his findings to language itself and concluded that metaphor (selection/substitution) and metonymy (combination/context) must be opposed as they were generated from antithetical principles. (Ferdinand de Saussure adopted this approach with his study of **paradigm** and syntagm.)

The idea that the forms of language are opposed rather than complementary not only found expression in French structuralism, but also in **psychoanalysis**, where the notions of 'condensation' and 'displacement' came to equal Jakobson's original **binary opposition**.

Methodology

The practices and techniques used to obtain information.

In social research methodology is used to refer to the processes and techniques by which information is gathered. Researchers can then use this information to validate theories about social life.

Historically sociology aspired to be considered a science and cultivated scientific methods in its research, methods known as quantitative, which typically involve the collection of large amounts of numerical data. By contrast, qualitative methods use small sample sizes and more detailed and subjective investigation. The divide between quantitative and qualitative approaches was once considered unbridgeable, but researchers now accept the relative values of both.

If methodology is the basic process of acquiring information and collating it, the real issue is the assumptions behind this process and the consequences they may have for the final outcome.

See also Behaviourism, Empiricism, Positivism.

Modernism

A mode in artistic practice that sought to rethink the individual in society. A style or 'structure of feeling'.

This term originally referred to the dominant tendency in twentieth century arts but now refers to that against which **postmodernism** defines itself. Modernism was a movement in cultural and artistic spheres that consciously set out to explore what the experience of modernity meant to those involved in it. Its basic premise was a rejection of traditional ways of seeing things, of traditional forms in music and art, and of accepted moralities and methods of explaining the world. Impressionism and cubism are good examples of modernism in the arts since their ways of representing the world are clearly, and sharply, different from the traditional realist forms. Modernism has been called the 'tradition of the new', which rather neatly captures its somewhat ambivalent place today.

Modernism continued an avant-garde elitism which rejected mass culture as well as **bourgeois** culture. Modernism was intellectual, urbane and an artistic practice of 'depth', of abstraction. Modernism was high culture, and Eurocentric in its outlook. From being a radical critique of bourgeois culture, modernism has become the nostalgic orthodoxy of cultural elites.

Modernism can therefore be seen either as a movement committed to certain principles in artistic practice, or simply as a historical epoch in which cultural production took on both a self-reflexive and critical outlook. Modernism is clearly related to a new 'structure of feeling' which developed in response to the rapidly changing nature of industrial society and of social and cultural relations within it. Modernist attitudes to modernity varied, however from the embracing of everything new and technological to a complete rejection of everything to do with what the poet T.S. Eliot described as the 'waste land'.

Moral panic

A media spiral in which social control and hysteria escalate social problems.

Used in **cultural studies**, this term was introduced by Stanley Cohen in *Folk Devils and Moral Panics* (1972) to describe the ways in which the media escalate, if not create, agenda-setting panics about particular moral issues. He highlighted the way the forces of social reaction and control combined to isolate and exaggerate deviancy through the media, defining certain groups as a threat to societal values and interests. He drew attention to the way the **mass media** policed available frameworks and definitions of deviancy and created public awareness of, and attitudes towards, certain social problems. In *Policing the Crisis* (1978), the Centre for Cultural Studies extended this analysis of moral panic to consider the way that the media created and amplified certain kinds of crime (for example, mugging) to create panic and a reaction to a perceived problem which began to affect other agencies of social control, like the courts and the police themselves.

The development of moral panic follows a pattern which begins with the creation of an identifiable problem after initial events have attracted media coverage. A media **paradigm** is then set up which encodes subsequent events. Once particular events are codified as newsworthy, the media seek similar events and begin to build out from the event itself to its wider social implications. Drawing on experts—sometimes called 'primary definers'—the problem is then linked to wider social disintegration and represented as being symptomatic of a moral crisis: media amplification is underway. The 'facts' reported by the media are increasingly framed by the moral panic and pressure is then applied to politicians and moral guardians to resolve the problem. The apparatuses of law and order and social control are drawn into the moral panic and react accordingly, often in the form of announcing emergency measures to deal with the 'problem'.

What the moral panic process demonstrates is that the media play a significant role in defining the moral and political agenda, and that the media have a commercialised interest in generating moral excitement. It is feasible to argue that whereas historically a moral panic was an isolated incidence of media behaviour, it is now the case that the media routinely and consistently sensationalise crime as a means of generating audience response and ratings success. Crime has, in fact, moved to the centre stage of the media agenda so that a virtual permanent state of moral panic exists in the commercialisation of deviance.

Multiculturalism

The celebration of cultural pluralism.

A term which became popular in the 1970s in the US to celebrate ethnic diversity. It was adopted in opposition to earlier policies of cultural assimilation, as represented by the 'melting-pot' **metaphor**. Governments in North America and Australia implemented multicultural policies as a form of social engineering which then came under criticism by the New Right, for example, Arthur Schlesinger, *The Disuniting of America* (1991). Multiculturalism has also been critiqued for ignoring the particular needs and circumstances of indigenous populations.

Myth

A set of fables or stories which explain origins.

The term was first used in English in the nineteenth century, and has since entered everyday language both as fable and as everyday urban myth. Its meanings are multiple and depend more and more upon the particular context in which it is used. Historically, it was first used to refer to 'fabulous narration' or imaginative constructions which were treated as historical myths or legends. Its secondary use was to criticise the idea of stories or legends which were untrue or untrustworthy. Both uses have persisted. Myth has always been opposed to truth or reality, but there has been a tendency which comes out of Romanticism to revalue myth as containing a higher level of meaning than everyday reality. Interestingly, Claude Lévi-Strauss and Roland Barthes have maintained this notion of myth as somehow being a particular mode of thinking that is different to the ordinary.

Myth can be seen as narratives of origin or, in other words, stories of the history of a **culture**. This is another way of saying that all cultures tend to create explanations of their becoming in order to justify their present, a kind of psychic fixing of cultural continuity by anchoring the present in the past. It is noticeable that all religions are heavily dependent on myth to sustain their ideological hold on the social patterns of communities. For Lévi-Strauss, myth was the mode in which primitive cultures thought their relationship to the world, to social relations, to marriage and to death. Thus myth was centrally involved in the **cultural reproduction** of a society's basic functioning and, for Lévi-Strauss, the analysis of myth and its structuralist patterns was the central aim of anthropology.

Roland Barthes famously updated Lévi-Strauss's analysis of myth to consider the cultural and ideological forms in which **popular culture** operated in capitalist society. In his *Mythologies* (1966) he argued that 'myth is a form of speech', by which he meant that myth was a particular way of understanding the world and of expressing it, and also that myth appeared to be natural, while in fact it was a means of making the ideological appear as the 'given'. Thus for Barthes, as well as for Lévi-Strauss, myth was a form of thinking which reconstructed the world in an acceptable fashion while hiding the contradictions and repressions that were a necessary part of a partial world view.

Nationhood

The idea of a nation state, of fairly recent historical origin.

The nation is one of those ideas that has become so familiar that it hardly seems to need explanation, which in one sense demonstrates how 'naturalised' an idea it has become. It is difficult to realise just how historically recent an idea it is though, and how specific the form of the nation state is. Nationalism, the pseudo-religion of nationhood, was responsible for a great deal of division, war and massacre during the eighteenth, nineteenth and twentieth centuries, and continues to be so. This is because the nation is almost always a contested term; whether it is based on ethnic groups, language, **culture**, boundaries, folklore or religion, there is rarely real uniformity within an artificially created state.

Nation states emerged out of the break-up of medieval and classical empires, some of which lingered on into the twentieth century, and the myths of nationhood can be seen as both responses to ideological uncertainty and as signifiers of ethnic and cultural bonding. It is interesting that one aspect of all nationhood appears to be the creation of 'myths of origin' which sustain and legitimise national sovereignty. Nowhere is this more apparent than in the case of Israel, a nation state that is barely 50 years old, created out of mainly occupied lands and utilising a notion of 'Greater Israel' drawn from the Old Testament.

The idea of the nation is regularly confused with the exercise of **power** by the nation state, which is a political and economic entity, and often the nation is thought to be created or renewed in war, a meta-symbolic fantasy which has had incalculable consequences.

See also Citizenship.

Nature

An all-encompassing term that refers to the 'natural', to a benign natural world or 'Mother Nature', or to a set of ideas about the natural world.

Like many recently contested ideas, nature is one of those concepts that has had a long and charmed life. A common-sense idea, it has been used uncritically since at least the time of the Greeks. In its earliest and uncontested uses, it simply referred to the wilderness, the non-cultivated part of the world unaffected by human activity. The concept implicitly included the entirety of ways of life which were dictated by natural rhythms and realities. Nature was opposed to **culture** or **civilisation** and seen as the force that directed the non-human world. Sometimes considered benign, 'Mother Nature' has often been conceived of as a quasi-religious entity which contains within it an implicit moral stance: some things are said to be 'against nature'. At the same time the idea of nature as 'red in tooth and claw' coexists with this feminisation of the concept of the natural, pointing to the ideological nature of the concept.

If nature was ever an uncomplicated idea, or one that could be uncritically used, it certainly is no longer. By extension, the idea of 'human nature' or of natural human behaviour has come under a great deal of scrutiny over the last 20 years or so. In the debates about human sexuality, the nature/nurture debate for a long time occupied central stage, depending on the idea of 'nature' as an unchallengeable force which dictated predictable forms of behaviour. In other words, the concept of 'nature' has provided an ideological building block in many areas of human thought, posed against 'culture' or 'civilisation' as a simple, all-encompassing entity as abstract as it is transcendental.

Neo-liberalism

The dominant economic model in the developed world since the 1980s.

Called variously neo-liberalism (Europe/NZ), **Thatcherism** (UK), Reaganism/Reaganomics (USA) and **economic rationalism** (Aust), this is a market-oriented approach to economics. Neo-liberalism is based on neo-classical economics and emphasises a minimal role for government, with market factors being the driving force in economic development. This has led to cutbacks in the postwar welfare state in most developed countries and encouraged the growth of a global economy. Liberty and free markets are the cornerstones of this reworking of classic liberalism.

Network society

Buzz term of the late twentieth-century information society.

Referring to much more than just a collection of motherboards and phone lines, the networked society is one in which a higher than previously possible level of connectedness between individuals is seen as both necessary and normal. It is always implied that more **communication** is better communication.
See also Cyberspace, Globalisation, Information revolution.

New age

A spiritual reaction to consumerism; a paradigm connecting the old and the new.

This is a portmanteau term that describes any of the new social movements and 'alternative' philosophies which have arisen in western society over the last two decades and which self-consciously seek spiritual enlightenment and political liberation. New-age philosophies and politics tend to be utopian, ecologically driven and to draw on traditional and primitive ideas of community in order to distance themselves from postmodern and consumer society. Eco-warriors who fight to preserve the environment against development and industrialisation are interesting examples of these new social movements.

At the same time there is a distinct media emphasis on new-agers as being a generation of narcissistic consumers. Another way of putting this is to say that it is a troubled concept which reflects a heterogeneous space in cultural conflict. Of course the strangest part of the new-age approach is that it almost entirely depends on old-fashioned points of view. Also, paradoxically, new-age books, videos, crystals and other aids to higher consciousness are very big business, or perhaps small community business on a large scale.

New historicism

Insists on analysing literature in historical contexts.

New historicism is a 1990s' movement which derives, unsurprisingly from historicism.

Historicists argued that historical analysis was the only valid method of investigating social and cultural phenomena. However, the observer's perspective would always influence the historical analysis.

New historicism is a method of reading literary texts in their historico-cultural contexts. It emerged in opposition to new criticism, which analyses texts as self-contained objects, independent of their cultural influences. New historicism has concentrated on the re-analysis of Renaissance, romantic and American literatures.

New man

A reaction to the 'third wave of feminism'.

A mythical character who demonstrates caring, shares emotions and child-care and who gives up his highly paid job to look after the children. Despite the fact that in some senses new men do exist, the media seem to simultaneously project and deride them. The instability of this idea demonstrates how threatening new men would be to the stable dichotomies of male/female. In an age of rapid transformations, new man can be seen as an object of scorn as the projection of fears about masculinity and its insecurities. As women and technology undermine the traditional idea of the male breadwinner, there is what is sometimes called a 'crisis of masculinity', or a reworking of social and gender roles. The new man can be seen as a projection of the possibilities of these changes.

New Times

A term used to describe the social and political transformation of the 1980s, sometimes referred to as postmodernism.

The **cultural studies** approaches of the 1960s and 1970s, which were profoundly influenced by the radical political attitudes of Marxism, came under sustained criticism during the 1980s when the rise of **Thatcherism** and New Right ideologies seemed to herald a new era: New Times. The postwar consensus of government intervention in the economy, full employment and tolerance of trade unionism gave way to the **economic rationalism** of completely free markets, state withdrawal and strongly anti-union policies. These New Times were seen to consist of both economic and social changes which found their expression at the level of **culture** and politics, changes which were seen as irreversible. At the economic level, New Times were characterised as post-Fordist, at the political level as post-class and at the cultural level as postmodern. Clearly what this intellectual intervention was expressing was some kind of sense that the world had taken a quantum leap into a new kind of socioeconomic reality, and this has certainly proved to be the case. During the 1990s the pace of economic and social change has accelerated to such an extent that Thatcherism itself now seems outdated, although economic rationalist ideas still hold sway in many countries.

The real difference between the New Times argument and the cultural analysis of **postmodernism** is that the former is firmly rooted in an analysis of the social and the economic, whereas the latter almost assumes that they are no longer relevant. The analysis of post-Fordism most clearly demonstrates the differences between the two, and in his article 'The meaning of New Times' (1989) Stuart Hall summarises post-Fordism as a restructuring of global **capitalism**, the key features of which are: multinational companies which diversify their interests and operate on a global basis; the development of 'new' service industries; and increased use of new technology to replace labour. The workforce which was traditionally based on unskilled male labour now includes more women, ethnic groups and part-time workers. **Globalisation** of markets and the financial system which supports them, with a corresponding loss of control by governments over their national economies is leading to the spread of wealth between the affluent parts of society and the new 'underclass' becoming more exaggerated.

Put another way, we can say that post-Fordist flexibility replaced the earlier economic model of **Fordism**, which relied on centralised and standardised mass production utilising a traditional male workforce and assembly-line techniques. In cultural terms, post-Fordism represents an era in which **consumption** becomes ever more important and in which commodities become ever more 'consumable' as cultural objects. New Times are almost coterminous with the rise of computing, the transformation of work and the irresistible rise of consumerism. Whether postmodernism is the cultural expression of New Times is a much larger question; at least the notion of New Times points fairly clearly to a socioeconomic transformation that has its roots in known social patterns, not in a philosophy of **deconstruction** and the hyperreal.

News values

The rules by which news stories are judged.

News editors are the arbiters of the newsworthiness of a story. The criteria they use in their evaluation include public appeal and whether or not running a story is in the public interest. Whereas issues of public appeal can be quantified objectively, to some extent, in sales figures or ratings, issues of public interest are much more subjective. However newsworthiness is not the only prerequisite for inclusion of a story in a news bulletin or publication; the interests of those who control the media can be a deciding factor. News values were historically assumed to be 'objective' but this idea is often criticised in media studies. *See also Agenda setting, Fake TV, Feedback.*

Nomadic theory

This is, as the name suggests, theory that is rootless, homeless or moves across disciplines.

This is an idea that is important in post-colonial and poststructuralist thought, in particular in its theorising of the nomadic subject which transgresses boundaries. It is an idea that comes out of the work of Gilles Deleuze and Felix Guattari, whose complex work in **psychoanalysis** and cultural theory is beginning to have a wider influence. The term probably comes from Deleuze's essay 'Nomad Thought' (1985) in which he argues that much of theoretical **discourse** derives from official state apparatuses and is therefore driven towards stasis and inflexibility. Nomadic thought, on the other hand, works to 'deterritorialise' forms of thought, to unravel and oppose dominant ideas and theories. Similarly, nomadic **subjectivity** is seen as fluid, transgressive and resistant to hegemonic discourses of fixity.

The idea has been taken up in feminist theory by Rosi Braidotti, who argues that it provides a means to go beyond phallocentric theory and to create new forms of female subjectivity. This has influenced thinkers like Donna Haraway and Luce Irigaray, who have explicitly set out to think of nomadic subjectivities which exceed the limitations of traditional thought. To be a nomadic subject is to be homeless, to exist in an imaginary and symbolic realm that subverts the accepted definitions of what is and replaces them with categories of fluidity and possibility.

See also Travelling theory.

Norm

Rules regulating our behaviour.

Eating breakfast, lunch and dinner is considered a norm in western **society**, so is having only one sexual partner at a time. One of these norms is adhered to more than the other, but which one? Norms are either customary behaviour within a given society or behaviour which is considered desirable by this society. Like all rule systems, norms are accompanied by rewards and punishments. Norms are learnt through socialisation, but this approach has been criticised for assuming that particular norms are universally accepted within the **subject** group.

See also Anomie, Functionalism.

Ontology

Does God exist? Do we exist?

Strictly speaking, ontology refers to the philosophical debate spanning many centuries about the existence of a supreme being. In broader terms it discusses the essential nature of all beings. We all *believe* that many things exist in the abstract rather than concretely. We would prefer to say we *know* this, and this is where ontology comes in. Ontology does not offer any easy answers but rather a framework for discussion for some of life's biggest questions.

Societies have shared understanding of the customs and mores that hold them together, not all of which are prescribed or even written. Would a society exist in the same way, or even at all without this abstract cultural framework? In the twentieth century W.V.O. Quine coined a **metaphor** of a 'web' of beliefs which ties societies together.

Michel Foucault drew on this idea for his theory of discursive formulae that limit permitted understandings from one utterance to the next.

See also Epistemology.

Orientalism

This general term was taken over and redefined by Edward Said, the Palestinian–American theorist of post-colonial **culture**. His 1978 book *Orientalism* has been very influential in shifting the focus of debates about the relationships between the East and the West, the Orient and the Occident. What Said was centrally concerned with was to think about the way that the 'Orient' had been constructed and represented—and hence controlled—by western modes of thought. This was very much in line with Michel Foucault's definition of how a particular **discourse** exists and functions.

Before Said's reconstruction of the term it had been used to describe those scholars and thinkers who studied the 'East' and its complex and different culture. Said's argument was that the discourse of Orientalism was deeply complicit with the imperialism that had brought it into existence, and was therefore theoretically and linguistically unable to break out of those complicitous relationships. The Orient was constructed in this discourse as the **other** of western rationality, as the binary opposite of the western notion of reason and control, and thus it was not possible to see the East in its own terms and complexity. Orientalism is fundamentally Eurocentric and historically racist, a position which post-colonialism, drawing on Said's analysis, has begun to deconstruct.

Later examinations of Orientalism have also considered the way in which notions of the Oriental 'other', the westerner, were also constructed within this discourse, and how elements of Oriental culture have infiltrated the West itself. The West's fascination with the East has resurfaced in new forms in the last two decades with the rise of the so-called 'tiger economies' and with what are called 'Asian values'.

Other *see* Alterity

Paradigm

A shared set of ideas; the dominant pattern of thinking at a particular time.

This term was introduced by Thomas Kuhn in his discussion of the patterns of scientific development, and has entered general **cultural studies** debates as a broad term to refer to the dominant ideas of an era, a group or even an intellectual movement. Kuhn was referring to the shared set of ideas and commitment which operated within a particular scientific community at a specific time—almost the rules of the game within a particular time-frame. Its use in cultural studies tends to be looser, and to include non-specific factors like context or ethos, whereas in **semiotics** the term is used to refer to a set of terms which constitute a group with an overall generic similarity. Although the shift from modernity to postmodernity is accepted as a paradigm shift, postmodern thinkers continually challenge the authoritarianism they consider encoded within the notion of paradigm. The term has also entered the general vocabulary where it is used in business and management discussions as well as in advertising and cultural analysis.

Parapraxis

The original Freudian slip.

The act of expressing subconscious thoughts and desires in a moment of weakness. It can also indicate a situation where there is a conflict between duty and **desire**. The term has been used in recent years (incorrectly) to mean 'paying lip service'.

Pastiche

The quoting, copying or imitating of the original to provide an inferior version.

According to Frederick Jameson, one of the features of **post-modernism** is the loss of originality or creativity, and its replacement by pastiche and reproduction. Throughout post-modern culture the old, the avant-garde and the historical are plundered for forms and ideas which are then recombined and reproduced as pastiche without the wit and **irony** that parody displays. Pastiche is a mono-linear reduction of all forms to a commodified pattern of entertainment and consumption, which is the dominant style of 'themed' restaurants, bars, clubs and shopping centres.

Patriarchy

A society in which the male/masculine is assumed as the norm.

Another important term used across the humanities and the social sciences, this concept comes out of the resurgence of feminist criticism. Its literal meaning is the 'law of the father', but it is generally used to describe any **society** in which male norms are taken to be natural and in which men's superiority is unchallenged. The fact of patriarchy, or sexism, is almost unchallenged today, except by those in the men's movement who claim that women now control the entire universe, and this has to be resisted.

Patriarchy can be defined as a society in which the male, or masculine, is given dominance simply by fact of its **gender**, and through representations in media, art, literature, **culture** and law. The Christian church is an interesting example; based in the Christian dogma of equality, it has cheerfully relegated women to a secondary place for two thousand years, and in the face of demands for women priests has mostly reacted with hysteria and threats of excommunication. This proves not only that the church is patriarchal but also that the psychological dimensions of patriarchy run very deep. **Feminism**'s response to patriarchy in the 1970s was the development of 'consciousness raising' and an attempt to create a vision outside of patriarchal dominance.

Patriarchy as a theoretical description of society has come under much criticism for its failure to describe how it came into being, and how it could be changed—in other words, for being somewhat essentialist in its outlook. It remains, however, a central concept in much feminist analysis of society, and of its attitudes and ideologies.

Phallocentrism

The privileging of the phallus, that is, of masculinity, in language and thought.

This is a term that comes from the work of Jacques Lacan and describes the patriarchal symbolic order through which **culture** is acquired, and which privileges the phallus as the primary

signifier. That is to say, the relationship to language which is unconsciously acquired by the infant as it enters the symbolic order through the acquisition of language is one that structures a privileging of certain masculine forms and terms. 'Feminine' is constructed within these discourses as lack, as **other**, as an oppressed term in the very nature of language, and it is this phallocentrism which has been deconstructed and opposed within much of feminist thought. Sigmund Freud himself came under scrutiny as a propagator of phallocentric **discourse**, and there is little doubt that his position on the nature of woman was that she was constituted as 'castrated', as lack. Phallocentrism has replaced the older term 'androcentrism' in feminist discourse and probably more specifically calls attention to the naturalised assumption of male superiority within culture as a whole. In its most general sense it refers to a description of the defining principle of patriarchal domination or, in other words, a system that uses masculinity as the **norm** and which defines femininity as being subject to masculinity, to the law of the father. To put this in linguistic terms, it means any system of representation which privileges the symbolic power of the male, of masculinity, and thus reinforces the conscious or unconscious dimensions of patriarchy. One appropriation of the term which particularly signifies its general meaning is the use that Carol Smart makes of it to signify the assumption that all sexual pleasure comes from penetration, thus equating the entire symbolic realm with the dominance of the phallus.

Phenomenology

A philosophical approach that concentrates on the meaning of experiences.

Phenomenology is generally considered to have been developed by Edmund Husserl, a German philosopher who was heavily influenced by the 'intentional psychology' of Franz Brentano. Husserl was interested in conceptualising the reality of our experiences in relation to things in the world and our perception of consciousness and objects in its purest form. The whole approach is neatly summarised by Husserl's slogan 'back to the things themselves', meaning that theories and ideas should be set aside and the object approached without any preconceptions. The aim is to reflect on the experience of the object, to strip away all presuppositions and to concentrate on the immediate experience. The program of critically thinking about our inner experiences of the world and of ourselves is a radical one, and it generated a critical awareness of being in the world. Phenomenology's critique of **empiricism**, of 'natural experiences', was important but its emphasis on the ego led to charges of solipsism. Phenomenology had a major influence on **existentialism**, and on theories of **subjectivity** and **identity**.

Pleasure

The seemingly obvious, but very difficult, question of the definition of pleasure.

There is a historical use of this term, mostly associated with Sigmund Freud and his 'pleasure principle', which relates to the way a newborn infant is guided by the pleasure principle in its search for satisfaction, and which later gives way to a reality principle. It is also historically true that ideas of pleasure have always been bound up with notions of morality and religious observance, the term 'puritanical' implying just such a repression and rejection of the idea of pleasure. In much literary and **cultural studies** this century, it was assumed that the purpose of art was a mixture of enlightenment and moral elevation, pleasure perhaps being admitted as an afterword. Only in very recent literary and cultural studies has the central issue of pleasure itself been addressed, particularly the question of sexual pleasure within feminist, gay and lesbian politics and theory.

Debates about **popular culture** have also necessarily addressed the question of pleasure and entertainment, since these are central functions of much popular culture. Some recent arguments about popular culture have tended to uncritically embrace pleasure, entertainment and productivity as being in themselves progressive, a position described as **cultural populism**. Consumerism and fashion are also sometimes described in terms of pleasure, and thus almost coterminously as worthy of recognition, but this position smacks more of the repressed puritan heritage of academic life than of a critical liberation of the senses.

Pluralism

The idea that all viewpoints may/should be equal.

Pluralism is the coexistence on equal terms of different groups (cultural, ethnic, political, sexual) in **society**. In political terms this is promoting heterogeneity over homogeneity to create a healthy society. In literary criticism those who follow the Nietzschean view that there is no single truth use pluralism to allow more than one interpretation of a work. This in turn has been criticised as a form of 'dumbing down' for judging all interpretations as having equal merit.

Political correctness

A media term for any anti-discrimination policies.

A much-abused term seen by some to epitomise the left-wing agenda. Based on the morally sound premise that no member of society should be judged or disadvantaged for reasons of birth, age, sex, religion, weight (you name it), in some cases the concept has been taken to ridiculous lengths to avoid offending a single member of society. Much children's literature has been either proscribed or rewritten to incorporate alternative familial groups; universities and public sector employers have lowered entry standards for minority groups; and you now have to think before you speak. Political correctness is probably a classic **moral panic**. Media attacks on 'political correctness' often serve a hidden agenda of traditionalism.

Political economy of the media

A mode of understanding how the media function as economic enterprises.

The power of the media in society is generally agreed to be formidable, and how it is exercised is a matter of great debate. Understanding how the media function in society is one of the central aims of **cultural studies**, and a political economy of the media is an approach which basically highlights how the media function as economic enterprises.

The fundamental argument is that since most of the media, particularly the electronic media, are privately owned and run for profit, this will affect those media's output and political position. At the most general level, this argument is true since all aspects of an organisation's control, structures and policies are determined by the fact that it is a commercial organisation, with commercial aims in mind. It is also clear that commercial media are likely to adopt a pro-business outlook in their behaviour, just as government-run media are likely to adopt a pro-government attitude. However, the argument advanced against a political economy of the media approach is that such organisations adopt an 'independent' editorial position and present a balanced view of society. Such an argument relates to the notions of **bias** and 'balance', and suggests that there is no conflict between profit-making and objective reporting of how society functions. Media studies historically developed around these arguments of the **power** exerted by the economic on the cultural, and the degree of independence and impartiality found in different media.

A political economy of the media derives from Karl Marx's analysis of the relationship between the economic **base** and the cultural **superstructure**, and asserts that certain forms of economic organisation will lead to certain ideological positions being reflected. Furthermore it is argued that the introduction of commodity relations into the media leads to a situation that the **Frankfurt School** described as 'culture industries', companies which produce news and information as commodities and package entertainment in order to sell to mass audiences.

Collectively, information, news and entertainment become a commodity, and creating audiences becomes the means to selling that commodity. Economic pressures inevitably lead to a conservative, pro-business approach in disseminating information as a product. The growth and dominance of large media conglomerates leads to 'concentration' in the media industries and the suppression of oppositional points of view. The control of the media by economic and cultural elites also leads to a narrowing of the news agenda—the political output—of media organisations. In recent years concerns with electronic media and increased profitability have produced the dominance of a small number of international media conglomerates who promote a particular, and limited, political point of view. Vertical and horizontal integration, the process of merging different aspects of media industries, has accelerated, leading to less and less competition, and therefore less and less diversity in the world media.

The dominance in the international marketplace of several international conglomerates, many of whom are based in the US, leads to a position where local, or even national, media coverage is replaced by global coverage of news and events from a particularly limited news agenda. The drive to seek global audiences also leads to the 'dumbing down' of media coverage and analysis. In a nutshell, the questions about the implications of this analysis for media output and audience consumption are hotly debated.

Polysemic

A property of signs/texts which can have multiple meanings.

This term refers to the way in which a **sign**/text can be ambiguous, generating many different kinds of meaning. The way in which messages are constructed, framed and delivered seeks to fix this possible polysemic trait and transmit a dominant meaning. Much of the work of the electronic media is precisely to control and fix messages within an acceptable **paradigm**— what are called **news values**—and to encode messages in such a way that make them unambiguous. The frame of reference of television news, in particular, is limited and repetitive, assuming a very narrow range of possibilities in explaining events.

Inter-cultural communication demonstrates that the meanings of any action or event are potentially multiple, and that thus polysemy is a natural condition of all communication. The importance of the idea of the polysemic in media and **cultural studies** is that it undermines the structuralist insistence that meanings are fixed by language or by the text, and that only one viewer/subject position is on offer.

Popular culture

Initially the opposite of 'high culture', then used to refer to 'mass culture', now simply 'popular'.

Rather like the notion of **culture** itself, this is one of those terms which appears straightforward but has a complicated theoretical usage. In the nineteenth century, 'culture' held an uncritical place as the 'best that had been thought and said' and was the culture of the **bourgeois**. There was a vague interest in what was called 'folk culture', the culture of the masses or of the rural peasantry, but this had no status. The social and cultural transformations of the early twentieth century, however, brought the masses onto the screen of history, and with them came major changes in culture and cultural perception.

The power of American industrialisation, the beginnings of commercial culture and the political threat of revolution and communism made the 1930s and 1940s great periods of change in cultural terms. In Britain the literary theorists F.R. and Q.D. Leavis began to analyse what they called 'mass culture' and to warn of its populist appeal and its threat of the 'Americanisation' of culture (F.R. Leavis, 1930; Q.D. Leavis, 1968). Popular culture was thereby branded as commercial, trashy, misleading and lacking in morals.

Using Marxist and Freudian accounts of domination and **ide- ology**, the **Frankfurt School** came to fairly similar conclusions, except that they were even more pessimistic about the effects of what they called 'mass culture' and the 'culture industries'. These kinds of critique have been fairly consistent ever since, although **postmodernism** has recently reversed this attitude, seemingly to celebrate popular culture. However, at the same time as the Leavises were attacking the rise of popular culture, Bertolt Brecht, the left-wing playwright and poet, was advocating a truly 'popular culture' which reflected the ideas and aspirations of the 'broad working masses' and which advocated progressive political ideas. These two opposing views of popular culture have structured the debate ever since.

In Britain the debate about popular culture shifted in the 1950s with the beginnings of what we now call **cultural studies**, particularly with the work of Richard Hoggart and Raymond Williams. They argued that an authentic working-class culture was just as worthy of analysis as 'high culture' or 'literature', and sought to promote proper analysis of popular cultural forms. This early phase of cultural studies, typified by Williams' *Culture and Society*, was rapidly overtaken by the arrival of **structuralism** and **semiotics**, as well as the perceived importance of Althusserian Marxism. The study of culture shifted to the study of the forms of ideology in popular culture, especially through the Althusserian **paradigm** of ideology as an 'imaginary relationship to the real'. In film and media studies this produced a good deal of work that looked at the way that media texts 'interpellated' the viewer within dominant ideology. Semiotic and Althusserian readings of popular culture produced a similar view of the 'hypodermic' effect, where ideology was injected straight into the head of the consumer and this closed world could not be broken other than through scientific readings of the text.

This high structuralist moment of popular cultural studies gave way to poststructuralist and postmodern readings that turned ideology on its head and began to celebrate the diversity, fecundity and carnivalesque nature of popular culture, finding resistance where Althusserians found interpellation. Within postmodernism, popular culture is elevated almost as an aesthetic in its own right, with Madonna as the queen. The politics of popular culture are complex, however, encompassing global media industries, mass consumerism, identity and the celebration of signification as endless possibility.

Positivism

The philosophical approach that advocates knowledge based on observation and experience alone.

Positivism is both the doctrine associated with the work of Auguste Comte and a wider approach to the sciences which is sceptical of all theoretical deduction and in favour of the positive accumulation of facts. Positivism began as a philosophy of science but became an **ideology** in the humanities, particularly in sociology and geography, where the idea of 'objectivity' and the importance of observable 'facts' became a doctrine.

The attraction of the scientific method in the humanities is partly to do with the empirically verifiable nature of its results, which gives a realist feel to the procedures of disciplines dealing with complex realities that are, in fact, changing, and are changed by, the role of the investigator. Objectivity has to take account of **subjectivity** in order to produce a proper picture of the humanities, and it is for this reason that positivism has been discredited in the social sciences. Positivism portrayed an empiricist approach to all subjects as being universally valid, and the production of verifiable evidence as also being the proper search for truth. This was the dream of a universalising method which reduced everything in the universe to 'facts', constructed 'laws' out of these facts and then tested the facts against reality, thus producing a unified and integrated single system of knowledge. That positivism clearly constructs the world in a particular way has become glaringly evident in much recent humanities debates and led to the positive discrediting of it as a partial ideology.

Post-colonialism

A theorisation of emerging cultures posited on overturning the colonial experience.

This term derives from thinking about the consequences of decolonisation, which developed in earnest after World War II and accelerated in the 1950s and 1960s. The question of the impact of colonial/imperial power on the people of the colonised nations is a complex and difficult one which involves not only economic exploitation but also psychological and cultural domination. The concept of post-colonialism relates to the attempt to disentangle this interaction of the 'colonised' and the 'imperial' subjects.

Although the western powers no longer directly rule many Third World countries, there is still a relationship of unequal power in which global capitalism exercises formidable influence over the destinies of formerly colonised countries, and this relationship is also at the heart of the post-colonial debate. Some theorists argue that in fact there is not a 'post-colonial' space which can be theorised in this manner, but at least the concept draws attention to the difficulties of thinking about current Third World/First World relationships. Under the influence of **poststructuralism**, post-colonial theory has set out to analyse the construction of colonial **discourse**, to deconstruct the imperial **subject** and to rethink the hybrid space that now exists within the post-colonial framework.

Post-feminism

The idea that feminism has been superseded.

This is another hotly debated concept, since one of its meanings is to imply that **feminism** either no longer exists or no longer needs to exist. It can be taken to mean either that most of feminism's objectives have been achieved—the liberal, optimistic version—or that they were misguided and have failed—the 'backlash' version.

In theoretical terms the concept is more often used to describe attempts in **cultural studies** to broaden the debate about the nature of **popular culture** to include an understanding of the sexual politics which underpin most cultural representations. As with **poststructuralism**, the emphasis has shifted from studying social structures or **power** relations to thinking about

culture, and the cultural representations of women, within a **paradigm** that assumes **identity** and **difference** are freewheeling possibilities.
See also Feminism.

Postmodernism/postmodernity

The successor to modernism or a new form of society, or a kind of poststructuralist philsophy.

This is one of the two or three most unstable terms in **cultural studies** and philosophy today. Its usages vary from simply describing what comes after modernism in the arts, right through to a claim that we live in a postmodern world which is completely hyperreal. It is also a term which has entered the broader culture and appears to have taken on a life of its own, so that it is much debated in the academy, gets used in the popular press and apparently represents a particular new philosophical position. The term appears to have first been used in architecture in the 1950s and 1960s, and was taken up by Jean-François Lyotard, who turned it into an anti-Marxist and poststructuralist critique of science and **society**. His 1984 book *The Postmodern Condition: A Report on Knowledge* seems to have set the seal on his appropriation of the term and to mark the birth of the theoretical movement we can now call postmodernism. It is necessary to point out that there is little agreement about what constitutes postmodernism, even as a theoretical position, but that one of the claims of postmodernism—that all theory occupies a relativist universe of possibility—means that even the grounds on which one would judge postmodernism are not clear.

A major feature of postmodernism is that it is strongly anti-foundationalist, which means that it denies that there are objective scientific truths and rejects **grand narratives** that seek to explain how society, history or science work.

The rejection of attempts to make sense of history or progress is extended in particular to a rejection of the **Enlightenment** claims for the powers of reason, science and scientific and technological progress. The philosophers of the Enlightenment—along with Immanuel Kant, Georg Hegel and Karl Marx—are all chastised for their naive and imperialistic, all-embracing theories of the world. The rejection of large-scale theories goes hand in hand with the celebration of fragmentation, **difference**, discontinuity and the ephemeral. Hence origins, continuity and unity in historical periods are seen as an illusion. Of course, this instability of meaning makes it very difficult to characterise the postmodern period itself, but this is not seen as a problem.

In place of meta-narratives, which are seen as no more than the legitimation of hierarchical **power** structures, postmodernism seeks to consider the immediate, the local, the marginalised in society, the micro-politics of power relations, or the social fragments of alienated youth or marginal groups. There is an implicit stance that the local, the fragmented, the fluid, the ambiguous has a privileged place in the analysis of society. Postmodernism is pragmatic, local and contextual. This radical scepticism about claims to truth extends to the argument central to **poststructuralism**, that language is unable to represent the world, or that there is any fixed meaning or truth. For the postmodernists, meaning is always deferred, fragmented, relational and non-referential, which leads to what is called a 'crisis of representation'. Jean Baudrillard also claims that the **sign** has been commodified, and that the **signifier** and the signified have collapsed into each other, producing a culture in which there are only signs; there is no depth and there is no **ideology**—nor, in fact, are there any subjects.

The individual in postmodernism is seen as an ideological structure, albeit one that has no false consciousness; it is simply consciousness, which is discontinuous, fragmented and unstable.

The subject is 'schizophrenic' but, in a typical postmodern move, this is not schizophrenia in the clinical or classical sense (the referent) but more in the sense of a disturbed, fragmented personality. The argument for this position stems from the argument about language, which is, as we have seen, non-referential and non-representational. The chains of linked signifiers which create meaning are seen as being disturbed and unstable, partly as a result of mass communications, and the **subject** is seen as unable to reconstitute these chains of signification, and therefore doomed to wander around in a fragmented, confused—we might say, schizoid—state. All time is present, all meaning is simply the experience of the present, and all **culture** and psychic life are simply the mode of being of the **mass media**. This is the 'society of the spectacle' as described by Debord and illuminated by Baudrillard.

Postmodernism exhibits a fascination with mass communications, new technology, the idea that mass communications dominate the economy (fundamentally an idea advanced by the **Frankfurt School**) and with the idea of an 'information' economy. **Globalisation**, satellite and computer communications are all seen as aspects of the postindustrial world that postmodernism inhabits. **Mass media** and the collapse of meaning have therefore produced a culture centred on immediate **consumption** and sensationalised impact, with a consequent loss of depth. The immediacy of electronic communication ensures that the surface of endless signification is seamless, while the problems of meaning and analysis are endlessly deferred. Postmodernism and consumption have become the same thing.

The dominance of electronic media, consumption and the society of the spectacle has led to the decline of the distinctions between 'high' and **popular culture**, to the erosion of the cultural authority of the elites and to the creation of a mass consumerist populist postmodernism. The boundaries between science/art/culture/popular culture are eroded. The populist marketplace of electronic consumerism has become global and represents a new phase in capitalist, or post-capitalist, development which is entirely dominated by pleasure, spectacle, consumption, parody, **pastiche**, **difference**, fragmentation and **irony**. Eurocentric and **androcentric** ideas are replaced by pluralist and progressive ideas, but the question remains as to whether this constitutes a new aesthetic. Some critics, like Frederick Jameson, argue that what is described as postmodernism is nothing more than the cultural logic of late capitalism. In his work *Postmodernism or the Cultural Logic of Late Capitalism* he argues that there is a culture that can be described as postmodern, but that this is no more than the commodified form of mass consumerism and the domination of media industries that describe it.

Feminism and postmodernism have developed an interesting partnership in the development of studies of change, of changing identity and of postmodern feminism, as seen in the work of Gayatri Spivak and Judith Butler, but the connections between **deconstruction**, **poststructuralism** and feminism are rather eclectic. As a theoretical movement that celebrates innovation, appropriation and the micro-analysis of social development, postmodernism offers interesting modes of theoretical work, but it sweeps the wider questions of its relationship to the social sciences and philosophy under the historical carpet, throwing the rug of **relativism** over the gap.

Poststructuralism

That which comes after structuralism, or simply replaces it?

The structuralist revolution which overturned Marxism and **humanism** in the 1960s argued for a scientific study of the formations of **culture**, and for a relatively rigid theoretical approach to the analysis of language and literature. By the 1970s this approach was beginning to be criticised from many sides, and poststructuralism can be seen as the amalgam of all of these criticisms.

Poststructuralism rejects the idea that meaning in language can be fixed, finalised or used to make meaningful statements about the world (the referent). It adopts a position that we can describe as 'textualism' which sees everyone as imprisoned in texts: there is 'nothing outside the text'. Importantly, poststructuralism rejects the idea that **grand narratives** can be deployed to explain the development of **society**. It also rejects the distinction between 'depth and surface' (for example, the Marxist idea of **base** and **superstructure**) and the idea that deep structures lie behind, or can explain, the surface. Poststructuralism rejects the idea of a coherent, rational subject as the guarantor of the meaning of statements, and also rejects the 'metaphysics of presence' which implicitly guarantees meaning in the older structuralist **paradigm**.

At the same time, however, poststructuralism is often conflated with **deconstructionism**, which sets out to demolish the **myth** of the fixity of meaning in language, and to argue for a radical textualism.

Poststructuralism includes Michel Foucault's ideas about **discourse**, discursive practices and **power/knowledge**, as well as the critical **feminism** of Julia Kristeva, the critical philosophy of Gilles Deleuze and the social theory of Jean Baudrillard. Like **postmodernism**, to which it is a theoretical counterpart, poststructuralism is difficult to define, multifarious in its analysis and centred on its promotion of the fragmented, the deferred and the immediate nature of discourse. Its central preoccupation is the rejection of the structuralist claims that ideas, discourses, representations or knowledge itself can be rigidly fixed and described through a structuralist set of rules. Poststructuralism is, then, a philosophical position which embraces openness, the

formless, the subjective and the spontaneous while refusing ideas of objectivity, truth or reality.
See also Deconstruction, Postmodernism.

Power

The ability to control or influence something or someone, whether legitimately or not.

Power can be force, violence, coercion, domination, influence, defining or **agenda setting**, and it is usually exercised by one group, or individual, over another. Since the 1960s the question of who exercises power over whom, and for what reason, has become a burning issue in global politics. Where once the exercise of power was seen as the prerogative of elites, it is now questioned at every level of **society**. Thus understanding what power is and how it functions has become an important debate in feminist and cultural studies. Like many other forms in society, power was historically exercised through consensus and cultural domination, and the very process of questioning power began the process of unravelling its traditional operation. Power has been theorised within sociology, within **cultural studies** and **feminism** and in the recent poststructuralist work of Michel Foucault.

The two main definitions of power in sociology came from a liberal and a Marxist perspective; the liberal approach considers decisions made by individuals as the basis of power relations, whereas in Marxist sociology power is seen much more as a structural relationship involving coercion, and as the product of the class structure of society. Max Weber's famous definition of power as 'the probability that one actor within a social relationship will be in a position to carry out his own will despite resistance, regardless of the basis on which this probability rests' is the best summary of the individualist tradition. In the Marxist tradition, power is seen as being the product of economic and **class** interests; as such it is seen as class, rather than individual, conflict. The conflict between individual **agency** and social structure relates to the debate about agency in social theory, but also impacts strongly on debates about **culture** and the media. Some theorists argue that the media exercise power without responsibility, while others argue that power is exercised through audience choice and the market.

In recent cultural studies Michel Foucault's work on power has received a good deal of attention. Foucault rejects traditional ideas about power, which he argues are based on the idea that power resides in individuals or classes, operates from a central site and is imposed from above—what he calls the juridico-discursive model. This notion of power is based on a repressive and antiquated model, as far as Foucault is concerned, and fails to incorporate the complexity of power as it operates in modern society. Foucault argues that power should be thought of relationally, as operating in a capillary fashion from below, meaning that it is dispersed throughout the social structure in multiple and polymorphous ways. Foucault sees power as operating at the level of everyday experience, mediated through individuals and discourses in which possible behaviour and understanding are constructed through the way that social discourses and technologies operate. Power is everywhere and is always productive, which means that people internalise discourses of power and **knowledge** and operate through them.

The idea of surveillance is important in this theory of power; perhaps self-surveillance would be the closest approximation of what Foucault is getting at. Foucault also talks about how institutionalised discourses control **subject** positions and possible actions, but again through a dispersed productive power. It is not clear how this notion of power, as always anonymous and fragmented, can be combated in any way, or even whether it needs to be. Power relations in postmodern society are undoubtedly complex, but the argument that power does not rest in elites or classes seems perhaps a little premature.

Psychoanalysis

A theory of the construction of human sexuality and its social consequences.

Psychoanalysis is always associated with the name of its found-ing father, Sigmund Freud, and has played an important role in theories of **gender**, of socialisation and in **cultural studies** generally. Psychoanalysis is both a theory of the construction of human sexuality and a practice of psychological intervention on an individualised basis founded on a 'talking cure'. Freud's social theories have been highly influential in the humanities, particularly in literature, art and media studies.

In understanding how the human infant is transformed into a gendered member of **society**, Freud opened up a whole new terrain of social theory, and gave great impetus to an under-standing of the construction of masculinity and femininity. However, his nineteenth-century scientific background led him to adopt certain biologistic positions in relation to masculinity and femininity which have been much criticised. The role of the unconscious in everyday life and the contradictory consti-tution of the **subject** in society—the realisation that the individual was not the rational subject of liberal theory but a bundle of contradictory impulses—were Freud's fundamental insights.

One of Freud's other central contentions was that civilisation required repression, that in fact society was founded on the repression of basic instincts, an idea which has great signifi-cance in social theory. Social control and social repression are key ideas in thinking about how a society functions, and how **power** is maintained, and Freud's ideas about group identity and the power of the father figure were demonstrated most acutely in the rise of fascism. The **Frankfurt School** took up Freud's ideas in social theory and applied them for the first time to the role of the media in society; their experience with the role of the radio in mass propaganda under the Nazis was highly significant here. Freud's understanding of symbolisation, the process in dream work where ideas or images stand for something else, influenced these theories of the media and of cultural production and **consumption**, throwing light on the way that **myth** and story influenced listeners unconsciously as well as consciously.

The individual in society is subject to many pressures. Consumer society in particular bombards the subject with images, advertising and entertainment devised to influence their behaviour in particular directions, and it is here that psychoanalysis plays an important role in theorising social behaviour and the media's impact on **culture** as a whole. The unconscious dimension of culture is vast and the strength of psychoanalysis as a mode of analysis is shown in the many revisions of Freud's original work and the widespread use of psychoanalytic concepts across media and cultural studies.

Jacques Lacan's reworking of the Freudian **paradigm** has been highly influential in the most recent phase of cultural, feminist and media studies, probably because of the way in which Lacan reconstructs Freud through a linguistic/structuralist framework. While remaining loyal to Freud's understanding of the centrality of the unconscious and repression in defining the basic operations of the human subject in society, Lacan conceives of the subject as being constructed in and through language. Lacan also centrally argued that the human subject was not, as was often contended, a unified being for whom analysis was a question of equilibrium, but was a subject divided against itself, a 'split' fractured being forever imprisoned in the limitations and excesses of language. Lacan's conceptualisation of the imaginary/symbolic/real has also been highly influential, as has his discussion of the mirror-phase.

Feminist cultural studies has engaged in a long debate with psychoanalysis about the constitution of masculinity and femininity, and with Lacanian notions of the how gender is constructed in language—what Lacan called the dominance of the phallus as **signifier**. Psychoanalysis has been a fundamental part of all discussion of sexuality and being in social theory, and its importance is hard to overstate, despite the fact that empirical psychologists have consistently attempted to rubbish it as unscientific.

Public/public sphere

The idea of a particular space of general public/political discussion or consensus independent of the state or ruling apparatus.

The idea of the public sphere refers to the creation of an alternative space for the circulation of ideas and information, separate to the absolute **power** of the **state** and to the realm of private existence. It is argued that this sphere developed in the eighteenth century and was constituted by the new **bourgeois** community of educated and critical writers, doctors, lawyers, scientists and journalists, motivated by the new **liberalism** and optimism of **Enlightenment** thought. The image of the new coffee houses of the period is often invoked to point to the new means of communication and dissemination of information which this new sphere represented. This new public sphere was a space that was critical of existing dominant political and social arrangements and offered a counterweight to received opinions and ideas. Out of this came the notion of 'public opinion' and, later, 'public interest' and 'public broadcasting'.

Queer/Queer theory

A 'non-straight', oppositional, non-essentialist approach to sexuality.

Queer is another recent concept which derives from a 1960s reversal and reappropiation of an established idea. Where homosexuality had previously been described as a perversion or as 'queer', the term was provocatively appropriated to describe a liberated refusal of normative heterosexuality. Queer was both a political reaction to oppression and a rejection of the normative binarism of 'heterosexual/homosexual'. Queer theory became a conceptualisation not of an oppressed separatist movement but of a group that was establishing differing forms of sexuality, contradictoriness, as normal. Sexual **identity** was no longer perceived as natural or fixed, rather it began to be seen as malleable, changing and diverse.

The term 'queer theory' began to be used in the early 1990s and allied itself with the poststructuralist and deconstructive breaking down of the essentialist categories which dominated much **cultural studies** theory. Queer theory also moved away from some of the **essentialisms** inherent in the idea of 'gay and lesbian' identities and also took up a critical stance in relation to feminist theory. Queer theory's commitment to deconstructing fixed identities has allied it to postmodern and eclectic modes of thought and has produced work across a wide range of humanities.

Race

An ideological construct in science.

Racial distinctions for example, 'Asian', 'Caucasian', 'Coloured' are seldom used in public except in tabloid journalism and police suspect descriptions. These appear to be obvious distinctions based on skin colour but they are not accurate, and the concept of race goes much deeper in representing myths of purity and separateness.

The biological definition of a race as a genetically distinct grouping of people must be blurred by historically high levels of interbreeding in most parts of the world. Distinctions such as 'black' and 'white' are no longer scientifically significant but carry important cultural overtones.

The term has been used interchangeably with **ethnicity**, especially by racists, but it is important to remember that ethnicity denotes a deeper level of shared cultural background than just a shared genetic pool.

The concept of racism has arisen because of the unfortunate human tendency to judge others by their physical appearance and way of life. The **other** is always perceived as threatening and many white supremacist groups base their thinking on nineteenth-century prejudices about 'uncivilised' peoples.

Racism is not confined to white supremacists. Rather, postcolonial thinkers argue that racism is embedded in all aspects of **culture**.

See also Alterity, Identity, Orientalism, Power.

Radical/ism

Pushing the boundaries.

Radicals typically challenge establishment figures and views. Radicals are not back-room players, they are out on the streets.

All social protest movements spring from radical roots, but have a tendency to lose their edge over time. The radicalism of the New Left inspired a generation of activists in the 1960s and 1970s, for example, gay rights, women's liberation and environmentalism, but most of these social movements have by now been incorporated (with varying success) into mainstream politics.

Other 'radicals':
Radical democracy: post-Marxists' term for a new left-wing politics which takes account of the rise of social protest movements, for example, gay rights and environmentalism.

Radical feminism: the insistence that the oppression of women is the main form of social oppression.

Radicalesbianism is concerned with sexuality and power, seeing sexual oppression as *the* oppression.

Reader-response theory

The death of the author has led to the rise of the reader.

In traditional literary criticism, the reader was almost completely ignored in favour of analysing the text and/or the **author**. This focus has shifted significantly in the last 25 years to a situation in which the role of the reader, or **audience**, has become almost dominant. This position ties in strongly with poststructuralist theory, which sees the author as simply one of the voices in the creation of meaning. Reader-response theory can be seen as an umbrella term describing several different approaches which all take as their central focus the role of the reader in creating cultural meanings. Historically, feminist literary analysis has argued that many texts construct an implied 'male' reader, and that therefore women either have to read as a male reader or adopt an oppositional point of view. Sometimes the term 'resisting reader' is used to describe the way in which someone appropriates a text in oppositional terms, refusing the dominant **encoding** or the implied message of the text.

What reader-response theory is looking at, then, is a series of ideas about what the notional reader may do with a text, an idea that itself comes in response to the structuralist idea that texts centre readers, or construct them through language. The rediscovery of the reader also recognises that texts are fundamentally polysemous rather than closed systems of meaning, and liberating the reader from their non-existence allows many different positions to be adopted towards texts. However, the difference between the ideal reader, who approaches the text with a model competence in terms of understanding, and the aberrant reader, who decodes the text in idiosyncratic ways, is not easily explicable in terms of the text.

In the same way that a psychoanalytic reading may look at the repressed elements in a text, so a feminist reading would consider the deeper ideological messages of a text from the point of view of an oppositional reader. These ideas of how readers liberate texts are also found, in a slightly different formulation, in Stanley Fish's notion of an **interpretive community**.

See also Interpretive community.

Realism

A very antiquated idea of representing the world 'as it is'.

This is an idea which has a very long history in literary studies, particularly in relation to the idea of the 'realist' novel, but it became a very contentious issue in cultural and media studies. It is a term that has mostly fallen out of use, particularly in postmodern theory, which claims that there is no 'real' to represent, hence realism is effectively an illusion.

At its most general level the question of realism was historically one which posed the question of how a work of art could represent the world. This reflectionist view of the relationship between art and the world assumed that there could be some kind of natural representation of reality, and that a coherent and well-formed work of art would achieve it. Throughout the eighteenth and nineteenth centuries, various naturalistic versions of realism were dominant in the visual and written arts, and carried over into many twentieth-century versions of conventional realism, particularly in film and television.

Realism, as the mimetic depiction of **society** or reality, has always remained a problem for the arts, since it is often one of its avowed aims. Many avant-garde and modernist approaches sought to convey reality through a self-conscious distancing or 'defamiliarising' of reality—what Bertolt Brecht called the 'alienation effect'—but the aim was still to capture some sense of reality. Documentary film engaged in many complicated attempts to recreate reality either through attempting to film it immediately as in cinéma vérité, or through a fragmentary, collage-like attempt to seize the underlying structures of reality. Realism became a hotly debated topic under the influence of linguistic theory, which claimed that since language constructed reality, it was no longer possible to have a privileged access to that illusory realm. Under the influence of **post-structuralism**, the search for realism has been replaced by a self-aware search for the kinds of artistic practices which convey the complex nature of artistry itself. Realism is a rather retired concept.

Received ideas

The ideas, or sets of ideas, dominant in a particular era.

All historical epochs are marked by a set of dominant ideas, of received ideas that come to be accepted as the 'truth', or what is sometimes called the dominant **ideology**. The strength of the notion of received ideas relates more to 'common-sense' approaches to the world, however; for example, the notion of **globalisation** is seen as an almost natural and inevitable process in current thinking. Similarly, in the nineteenth century the received ideas about **race** and **colonialism** were uncontested:

the idea of empire seemed as natural as the idea that women were the weaker sex. Such ruling ideas have a historical dimension to them and a 'naturalness' that only become evident from a later, or critical, perspective. It is also often the case that in academic disciplines there are certain received ideas which tend to become an orthodoxy until they are challenged by new thinkers.

Reductionism

A pejorative description of theories that simplify the world.

Reductionism is the sin of simplification, one of the worst things that one can be accused of in the postmodern world. Put theoretically, it is any theory which explains all attributes of whatever is being studied by reference to a simple, or a number of simple, factors. Thus the claim that all forms of electronic entertainment are driven by the desire to maximise profits would be described as economically reductionist. Marxism is often accused of being reductionist in its attempts to explain everything as being the reflection of the workings of the economic base (see **Base/Superstructure**). Similarly, **sociobiology** is reductionist when it attempts to describe all human behaviour in terms of genes. Some feminist arguments about **patriarchy** can also be said to be reductionist in that they posit a single essence as the fundamental cause of all other phenomena, a theoretical position which is highly untenable. **Technological determinism**—the idea that all social change can be ascribed to technological change—is similarly reductionist. Causality is almost always a complex factor and, particularly in **cultural studies**, it is rare that any cultural phenomenon can be analysed in a reductionist fashion. It is an interesting question as to whether **structuralism** is reductionist in that it attempts to reduce all **culture** and being to the operations of language.

Relativism

The rejection of the idea of fixed, absolute points of view outside of position or context.

Relativists argue that there is no such thing as 'objective knowledge'; there are simply viewpoints from which discourses or forms of thought are constructed. Scientific knowledge, for example, is seen as being socially constructed, not simply discovered as true 'facts'. Much of postmodern thought is relativistic in its approach, rejecting the notions of truth, objectivity or absolute knowledge in any form. The rejection of objectivity, of the existence of ideas, knowledge, truth or categories which exist independently of the speaker, or point of view, is the fundamental characteristic of relativism.

Reflexivity

Self-awareness.

A dictionary definition of reflexivity is 'the property of referring to oneself'. In cultural theory, therefore, a reflexive approach allows a theory to incorporate a discussion of its own position and cultural construction in its findings.

Representation

The way in which meanings are depicted and communicated.

The fact of representation is so basic that it is often taken for granted, as is the idea that the world can be represented in a fairly straightforward way. It was often said in the nineteenth century that the novel 'held up a mirror to reality', which very much reflected the naturalistic view of **realism** that was a commonplace of all criticism. These common-sense approaches to the world and its representation have come under sustained attack by structuralists and poststructuralists.

Historically there have been two opposing views of representation, the first claiming that the world is amenable to representation and the second broadly rejecting the notion of the 'real', arguing that there is only the representation of representation. It is sometimes claimed in present-day **cultural studies** that there is a 'crisis of representation', by which is meant that there is an increasing awareness that the representation—or reporting, or describing—of something also involves placing, fixing and controlling it. Thus to talk about 'Third World' cultures in a particular way can be seen as an act of cultural imperialism, of **appropriation**, of exercising a western politics of representation.

Poststructuralism takes up this argument about the difficulties of representation and suggests that there is in fact no prior event or reality but only the process of signification itself. In **deconstruction**, the very fixity and possibility of creating meaning and representation are challenged and the anti-realist position is dominant: there is nothing other than representation (sometimes called re-presentation).

Stuart Hall, among others, has suggested a way out of the **binary opposition** of representation/realism by putting forward what he describes as a constructionist position. This approach argues that things don't simply mean by themselves but are constructed using representational systems, signs and concepts. This is to argue that there is no simple reflection, no basic correspondence between representation and the world, but a referencing, a signification that refers to a shared experience of the real world. Representations construct the world but they do so within a limited **paradigm** that makes them coherent, if debatable.

Risk/risk society

If you can't stand the heat, get out of the kitchen.

The risk society is a 1990s concept most vocally expounded by German sociologist Ulrich Beck. He argues that the risks of pre-industrial societies were known/believed to be either random acts of nature or God, while post-industrial society has created its own risks, through pollution in particular. Right-wing governments have adopted this perspective enthusiastically as it allows them to make the individual responsible for their own health and general welfare.

Self

'Do not ask me who I am and do not ask me to remain the same ... ' Michel Foucault.

The self, **subject** and **subjectivity** are closely connected.

Many theorists see the self as an autonomous and self-motivating subject, capable of real self-knowledge. Freud de-centred the classical liberal idea of the self, but psychoanalyst Jacques Lacan was the first to outline the classic **binary opposition** between subject and object in which he viewed the object as, simultaneously, gratification of the subject's **desire** and the actual cause of that desire.

The commonsense understanding of the self comes from **liberal humanism** and the belief that the self is endowed with the power of reason. Even universal sceptic René Descartes never doubted his capacity of reason. Liberal humanists also believe the self has a unified and unique **identity**.

For sociologists the concept of the self is more personal. It is a perception of who we are in relation to other people and **society**. Self-concept is the set of ideas and feelings which make up our identity, often drawn from our **culture**. For example, a new mother judges her performance by her cultural understanding of the role of 'mother'. Self-concept is the mental partner of self-image. Advertising in the **mass media** has a huge influence on the self-image of young people and is blamed for conditions such as anorexia nervosa.

Structuralists see the subject as the product of language and **ideology**, while postmodernists see it as a bargaining chip of relations of **power**. However, both aproaches agree that subjectivity is created by social forces and relationships.

Semiotics/Semiology

A science of signs; the study of how signs operate in society.

Semiology has passed from being a radical keyword of the 1970s to being one of the objects attacked by **poststructuralism** in the 1990s, as well as being an accepted part of the intellectual universe of the humanities. In present-day usage of the almost interchangeable terms, the notion of the semiotic has been complicated by the way that Julia Kristeva and others have appropriated it to mean the pre-linguistic phase of child development, and the indefinable elements of the **chora** associated with it. Historically, Charles Pierce actually used the term 'semiotic' to describe his study of signs in the nineteenth century, and the Swiss linguist Ferdinand de Saussure used the term 'semiology', but semiotics seems to have become the favoured term.

Saussure famously drew attention to the way language worked as a system, rather than considering its general historical development, and this led to a great deal of attention being paid to how signs work within the language system. Saussure revolutionised the study of language and also set the preconditions for the development of semiotics, and of course **structuralism** in general, which is intimately related to semiotics. As a science of signs, semiotics concentrated on the complexities of signification within **culture**, and on the way that language served as the model for all signifying practices.

It was Roland Barthes who introduced the distinction between the connotative and the denotative aspects of signification, and revitalised the project of a social semiotics in his *Elements of Semiology*. In all his work he drew attention to the way that signification was imbued with ideological and mythical elements, with the cultural dimensions of thought and language, not just the literal meanings of signs or words. This approach, which clearly aimed at drawing out the construction of meaning in culture through a signifying system that was not overt or consciously created, was highly influential in **cultural studies**, in film and media studies, and in the reworking of literary and artistic theory.

Sign/signifier

The elements of language.

French structuralist Ferdinand de Saussure saw the sign as the basic unit of meaning in language, whether written, oral or implied. He divided the sign into two components: the signifier (the physical form that we can see or hear) and the signified (the concept or object to which it refers).

Signs only function because of an arbitrary relationship which is culturally imposed. Barthes' classic example is that of a rose. A rose is normally a flower, but if a young man gives a rose to his girl, it becomes a sign of his romantic interest in her.

Signs can only be understood fully in relation to other signs belonging to the same system.

Jacques Derrida felt that Saussurean practice favoured oral over written communication. To this end, he developed the science of grammatology based on the principles of **deconstruction**. Deconstruction reveals hidden and subsconscious meanings

in texts, thus undermining the sign's status as the most stable element of language.
See Deconstruction, Semiotics.

Socialism

Worldwide workers' movement.

The modern origins of socialism date back to the English Civil War (seventeenth century) but as it is used now the term is a combined product of the **Enlightenment**, the French Revolution and the industrial age. Early socialist thought was primarily utopian, but the first mass working-class movement to express socialist ideas was the English Chartists in the 1840s. Karl Marx and Friedrich Engels formulated a more precise version of social-ism, but the Russian Revolution of 1917 led to a split between communism and socialism, communists considering socialism to be a middle stage between the proletarian revolution and the ideal communist state. Outside the confines of communism, socialism is associated with reformist left-wing politics.

Once as feared and derided as communism, socialism was the philosophical basis of many post-World War II welfare initiatives, such as free schooling and medical care. From the end of the twentieth century, political parties traditionally considered to be socialist (such as the British Labour Party and the German Social Democrats) began to espouse **neo-liberal** economic and social policies that their socialist forebears would have con-sidered capitalist.

Society

Patterns of social organisation within a state or nation.

'Society' is a construct and can take many different forms. On the most basic level it is a social system made up of both organisational structures (hospitals, prisons, schools) and social groupings (families, communities, ethnic minorities). Society can be theorised as a concept, but most approaches either consider particular aspects of the function of society or consider different national societies.

Traditionally members of a society were expected to conform to certain rules of behaviour as well as work towards common goals. Modern research, however, reveals an increasing diversity within even the most traditional of societies. It can be argued that the spread of electronic communications, free trade and other aspects of **globalisation** have possibly made redundant the traditional construction of society as confined within the nation state.

Former UK Prime Minister Margaret Thatcher famously once declaimed 'there is no such thing as society'. This reflects the **neo-liberal** view that only individuals and groups exist. One must note, however, that this viewpoint promotes the importance of **nationhood**, itself a form of society.

Sociobiology

A theory that seeks to explain all behaviour with reference to basic biological factors, like genetic make-up.

This is a term which has gained a good deal of credence in the last two decades, and has even made claims to be a discipline in its own right. It is best known through the work of writers like Edward Wilson, whose 1975 *Sociobiology: The New Synthesis* is the founding text. The ideas of sociobiology have received a great deal of media coverage and support, perhaps because of their innate simplicity and their appeal to right-wing theories of the inevitable brutishness of life and a Darwinian belief in natural selection and ethnic characteristics.

Sociobiology's approach is to argue that all forms of social behaviour can be explained through reference to biology, and in particular to the genetic make-up of the individual. Thus it is announced with some regularity that a 'gene' has been discovered which accounts for homosexuality, alcoholism, promiscuity, football hooliganism and, latterly, poverty and laziness.

Perhaps the question about sociobiology is really one of why there is so much media interest in a topic that is overtly reductionist, simplistic and unprovable. In a world where biology hardly seems to matter any more in terms of reproduction or sexuality, it seems odd that a theory which asserts that all behaviour is biological gets so much attention. This culturally brings us back to the question of **reductionism** and to the kinds of psychological reassurance that it provides in a fractured, post-biological universe.

Space

A key term in recent debates, which can be conceived of relationally, metaphorically or in imaginary terms.

Theorising space within **cultural studies** is essentially about thinking of it as a variable in shaping human activity and **culture**, and the city has been an important locus of that thinking this century. How the **subject** organises himself/herself in spatial terms within a **society** in which such relations are a matter of **power** has become a critical question in much recent cultural studies work. Our conception of space, the argument goes, has been radically altered: a 'time–space' compression has occurred creating a new mode of experiencing the social world in which we live. How to place oneself in a world that becomes ever more complex, global and spatially

233

disorientating is an issue that cultural studies, and particularly human geography, seeks to confront, finding a postmodern hyperspace in place of the ordered rationality implicit in modernist views of the world. It is argued that modernist approaches aimed at an integrated, controlled relation between buildings and their environments, rather like large housing estates that were planned to operate in logical patterns, while postmodernist approaches, on the other hand, are eclectic and unintegrated. Space, and spatial relations, are a question across all disciplines and there is a problem in the wide application of such concepts: there is almost no limit to the use of the term, from personal space through hyperspace to the reconceptualisation of space in physics.

Historically, geography has been concerned with space, and with thinking about it as a set of relations, of material things within a codified framework, but only recently has human geography developed ideas about space that take account of its relativity and social construction.

Marxist geography puts forward the argument that the spatial organisation of society is a consequence of capitalist social relations, at its most obvious in the spatial arrangements of **class**, city and living space. Henri Lefebvre introduced the idea of 'living space', which he saw as the actually and 'socially created spatiality' of society or, in other words, how interpersonal space is constructed by society. **Class** is seen as an important factor in terms of access to spatial resources and capitalism commodifies space just as it does other aspects of all social relations. Post-Fordist social relations of flexible accumulation and work practices are seen as restructuring the movement of people and forms of employment, as well as information and **culture**. Lefebvre also uses the term 'spaces of representation' to refer to the struggles of everyday life against enclosing conventions. Michel Foucault laid out the idea of a spatialised history, one that paid attention to thinking of the history of discourses and **power** in their spatial relations. Foucault (1986) argued that 'a whole history remains to be written of spaces' and his particular approach emphasised the connection between space and power, as for example in his well-known discussion of the panopticon.

Some critics, like Fredric Jameson, have argued that the transition from **modernism** to **postmodernism** can be located as a shift from concerns about time and temporality to a dimension in which categories of space are now all important. He argues that we exist in a decentred 'postmodern hyperspace' which effectively has no bearings and in which the subject feels adrift, itself an image of the **self** in a global world of flow and monstrous multinational information systems.

Feminist understandings of space see it as a gendered reality; public space has historically been constructed as a masculine sphere, and women can be seen as 'out of place' in the public domain. Suburbanisation can be seen to further construct this divide between women, the home and the public sphere: the suburbs are the sphere of the domestic and the city is constructed around public, masculine space. Some feminist theorists have also counterposed a feminist understanding of space as being fluid, dynamic and uncontrollable against a masculine dimension of space which is planned, controlled and dominated. There is, then, a hierarchy of space, of spatial relations and spatial definitions.

In recent years the control and domination of space has become increasingly political as richer communities in cities and suburbs seek social exclusion, or to create spaces of exclusion. Apartheid in South Africa was a conscious policy of social and political exclusion, a spatial configuration of domination, and yet the unconscious dynamics of these kinds of policies are still operating in many societies. Space may well prove to be the final frontier in sociopolitical thinking.

State

An embodiment of power, nationhood and sovereignty over citizens.

The state is notoriously difficult to define, being neither reducible to government and administration, nor to a geographical nation. At the same time it cannot be separated from either.

People commonly confuse state and government, and the terms are often used interchangeably. However the state is a social institution bearing the blueprint for the successful operation of certain functions. For example, maintaining law and order, resolving disputes, providing health and education services and defending its inhabitants. A government, on the other hand, is a collection of individuals, occupying positions of **power** and accomplishing some of the tasks necessary for the smooth running of the state. (Bear in mind, though, that this is only the theory.) The state will outlast its governments.

The state has traditionally been the custodian of legitimised violence. This has been critiqued on ethical, sociological and political grounds.

See also Power.

Structuralism

A theoretical movement that sought to reconceptualise all human society as the product of underlying deep structures.

This is a term which, like many others in current use, is extremely broad and covers several different bodies of theory. It is mainly used to refer to the body of postwar work which developed out of Ferdinand de Saussure's linguistic theory and which was further developed in France by Claude Lévi-Strauss, Roland Barthes, Louis Althusser and Jacques Lacan, among others. The widespread use of linguistic theory in many humanities disciplines means, however, that there is a great deal of overlap between structuralist and semiotic approaches. Furthermore, there is a brand of structuralism that developed out of the work of the Prague school of linguistics (see **Formalism**) in the 1920s and 1930s, which has also been incorporated into modern structuralist and poststructuralist approaches.

In sociology, structuralism refers to any approach that believes in the existence of social structures, like **class** or caste, and argues that social structure comes before the individual, and is therefore determinant. The French structuralist movement, while sharing the theory that structure precedes the individual, advocates a rather more complex theory of structure and **knowledge**. Modern structuralism, developed by the anthropologist Lévi-Strauss but based on the linguistic theory of Saussure, has grown to encompass literary theory, **cultural studies**, media studies, sociology and much of humanities, as well as having an influence on criminology and some physical sciences.

Structuralism's main claim is that there are formal structures which operate as invisible logics below the surface of language and **culture**. Understanding the formal rules of cultural systems, like language, provides us with a grammar of cultural rules that allows us to analyse the possible permutations of cultural output. Based on the 'linguistic turn' in the 1960s structural linguistics argued that culture, **myth**, **ideology** and even the unconscious (and the mind) were structured like language. Thus the model of language and how it operated was the model for all cultural analysis. Based on the assumption of **binary oppositions**—nature/culture, male/female, cooked/uncooked—structural systems of relationships were developed. The model of analysis—language—was extended to all cultural forms, including the media, literature, **popular culture**, art, wrestling and so on, with the consequence that a rather formulaic set of results were produced.

Structuralism is as all-embracing as it is controversial, and it makes very grand claims to explain all human activity as being constructed, but often fails to deliver much more than an insistence on formal structures rather than on intent and meaning. Structuralism is deeply anti-humanist, which is to say that it rejects the ideas of **subjectivity** and **agency**, and replaces them with the idea of language speaking through man (and woman). Structuralism's central claim is that human **culture** is only comprehensible through understanding its interconnections (or structures). The argument is that local variations of a culture, the particular myths or stories, simply reflect deeper structures which are constant laws. Discovering these constant laws is structuralism's scientific aim, and some would argue its great pretension.

The central questions become: what is a structure and where do structures come from? Are they timeless and ahistorical, and can they change? The most cynical critic might argue that structuralism does away with the messy complexities of human history and action, replacing them with a theoretical **paradigm** that is self-contained and unverifiable. If indeed all human action is determined by structural realities that lie outside of it, how would it be possible to move outside of those determinations to criticise them?

Subaltern

The underclass; the oppressed in colonial societies.

This is another term, derived from the work of Antonio Gramsci, which has gained significant currency in post-colonial studies. What Gramsci meant by the subaltern classes were those, like the peasantry, which existed in the workforce but which were denied representation in the wider cultural and political sphere. Because they lacked access to the hegemonic modes of educational and political domination, their voices were simply erased, written out of the prevailing news agenda. Put another way, the idea of the subaltern describes the study of history from the bottom up, rather in the way that some English Marxists—E. Hobsbawm and E.P. Thompson, in particular—studied history from the point of view of the working classes.

Subaltern studies emerged recently out of Indian historical studies and seeks to replace work that contests both colonialist and nationalist approaches, while also bringing into question the dominance of western intellectual thought in general. Through a journal called *Subaltern Studies* there has been developed a serious movement to recover Indian history from its colonial past, to rewrite history from a non-official point of view. The central point about the subaltern classes is precisely that they exist as the unspoken, the unthought, of **state** culture, and their history in reality is just as complex and interesting as the dominant, recorded groups. Just as **feminism** has recovered the silent history of women, so the subaltern approach has rediscovered the real history of those oppressed groups whose oppression is as much representational as it is economic. Seeing history as the preserve of elites and important individuals is a form of symbolic violence which reproduces the historical violence by which those elites maintained their absolute power.

Gramsci's initial understanding of the subaltern classes was to consider them in their active or passive relationship to the dominant class formations, and to consider the ways in which that relationship was negotiated—that is to think about the **culture** by which they lived their relationship to oppression. Subaltern studies picked up on this understanding of history from underneath, a history which is not only repressed but denied as existing at all. The subaltern group exists as the opposite of the elite and is, at some level, the condition of their existence, and it is this that makes a 'politics of the people' a necessity not just a theoretical possibility. Resistance to the dominant group is the key factor in the existence of the subaltern, and Gramsci's original approach was entirely justified in speaking the unspeakable.

In post-colonial studies, the term has the same resonance: it describes those who are oppressed by the terms of cultural discussion. The Aborigines in Australia provide one of the most acute examples of the reality of the subaltern. Their history was entirely hidden for two hundred years and they had no access to the formal languages of cultural description or complaint. Only in the last 20 years has the language existed to describe their non-existent state.

Gayatri Spivak has attacked the subaltern school for what she calls their essentialist position, their claim that the 'subaltern can speak', by which she means that the subaltern is always implicated in the colonial history of the oppressors, but this seems in itself to merely reproduce the idea of domination, of control. Subaltern studies promises to be a dynamic feature of post-colonial studies.

Subcultures

Cultural groups, often class-based, that express opposition to the dominant culture.

The concept of subculture grew out of a phase of the historical development of **cultural studies** during the 1970s and is a term that has partly fallen out of use as the mainstream culture itself has fragmented into more and more interlocking subgroups. The earliest work on subcultures within the culturalist tradition focused on the Teddy boys of the postwar era and looked at the way in which such groups expressed 'symbolic resistance' to their **class** experience and their experience of cultural oppression. Since cultural studies derived from a theoretical approach that wanted to broaden the scope of academic study of how **culture** functioned, it was a natural progression to begin to consider the subcultures of groups who were marginalised in **society**.

This political approach to considering culture meant abandoning the dominant ideological notion that working-class culture was naturally inferior and adopting a view that encompassed all cultural forms as expressing potentially critical elements and symbolic forms of 'making sense' of the world. Subcultures were defined as the reaction of particularly working-class groups, typically male, to the conditions of their oppression and exclusion from dominant cultures. Put most simply, the culturalist approach to subcultures was to see them as the way in which working-class youth expressed their dissatisfaction with their class experience.

Subcultures were a historical phenomenon in that they allowed young people to express their **alienation** from traditional family and class structures; an alienation partly brought about by new-found economic independence and new forms of media and cultural communication. Subcultures represented new forms of intentional communication among groups who were distancing themselves from dominant cultures and expressing their 'symbolic resistance' through clothes, style, language and behaviour. It is not surprising that the dominant culture found these new subcultures threatening and dangerous. At the same time, subcultures had to draw on the dominant culture and it is here that Claude Lévi-Strauss's notion of **bricolage** becomes important: members of subcultures took what was available and reconstructed it into patterns that reflected their dissatisfaction and rejection of dominant cultural meanings. One of the problems of the analysis of subcultures is its celebration of the way in which they rejected other groups, since often this celebration of identity involved violence towards others, the 'non-group'. Another central problem pointed out by feminists within cultural studies was that the analysis of subgroups almost always concentrated on males, marginalising women in exactly the same manner as the dominant culture.

Subject/subjectivity

The individual/the individual self separated from the world.

There is probably no other term that creates so many problems across the theoretical terrain of **structuralism**, **poststructuralism** and **postmodernism** than that of the 'subject', now often put in inverted commas to demonstrate its uncertain status. The individual subject as a concept now has a contradictory place in the analysis of **society** and **culture**. The subject seems to be the individual person who acts in society, but across the humanities there are competing theories that want to place the subject as the product of forces which are over and above the individual. The subject was originally conceived as contained within the **body** and separated from the **other**, but Sigmund Freud problematised that sense of coherence from which the subject as a concept has never recovered.

Karl Marx had earlier claimed that the worker in **capitalism** was an alienated subject, estranged from his/her 'species being' or essential nature, a split that would only be reconstituted by the abolition of private property and capitalist social relations. Marx argued that the subject was constituted by the ideological forces of capitalist society and therefore was the victim of illusion as to its role in society, an argument that persisted in many different forms throughout the nineteenth and twentieth centuries. Marx and Freud saw the subject as being conditioned by forces outside itself, and thus a kind of social construct, a category that was no longer self-aware. The subject was seen as 'decentred', as a contradictory reality.

This sense of the subject as the product of social discourses was taken up in structuralist approaches where, particularly through the work of Jacques Lacan, the subject was seen as a construct of language. Louis Althusser talked about the way that the subject was created in capitalist society through a process of (mis-)recognition, based in the psychic development of the infant (see **Psychoanalysis**). Althusser (1970) described this process as the **interpellation** of the subject, the hailing or address to the individual in which the subject mistakes itself as the coherent object of ideological structures. This is a complicated idea that implies that the subject lives out an 'imaginary relation to the real' in which they feel safely ensconced within ideological structures that position them as illusory agents. The structural determinism of this position was heavily criticised in later years but was the basis on which a lot of work on the subject in **cultural studies** was conducted, particularly in film and media studies.

Feminist critiques of the notions of the subject were concerned to develop ideas which understood the construction of masculinity and femininity, but which also gave space to the possibility of the redefinition of the subject. This concern with **agency** led to a rejection of Lacanian and other structuralist notions of the subject as the fixed product of other discourses, and sought a critical engagement with psychoanalysis which accentuated the (re)creation of feminine subjectivity. Julia Kristeva emphasised the 'subject-as-process' and many variations of **feminism** have sought to develop a theory of subjectivity that combines the linguistic theories of Lacan and the discursive approaches of Michel Foucault. The poststructuralist approaches to the subject tend to see it as a fluid possibility, something that is always becoming, through **identity** rather than through fixed subject positions.

Throughout all of these recent theoretical positions, however, the one common thread has been the dethroning of the idea of the coherent rational subject.
See also Self.

Sustainability

We are finally waking up to the fact that our global resources are limited. The concept of sustainability is drawn from the environmental movement and increasingly used in economics and management. It reflects a concern to husband resources wisely and to manage production and organisations in a self-perpetuating fashion.

Symbol

A sign, an image, a word or object that represents something else.

A symbol is anything that represents something else, and since Sigmund Freud's work on dreams and the unconscious, we are very aware in **cultural studies** that symbolisation is a central feature of psychic and representational activity. Freud pointed out that in dream work and repression, feelings and emotions become attached to other objects or images, which in turn become, through condensation and displacement, symbols of those displaced feelings. In all human creative activity, symbolisation is one of the primary means whereby cultural representations are created; in painting, in poetry and in music, the process whereby one thing comes to represent another is fundamental.

Since Freud we have been aware of the power of symbols to evoke unconscious resonances, and this is particularly true in any analysis of advertising, which relies fairly heavily on the motivation of unconscious impulses, like fear, attraction, guilt and desire. In an image-saturated society, understanding the functioning of symbols becomes steadily more important. Roland Barthes, the French semiologist, extended this kind of analysis to consider how particular signs worked, his analysis of a black soldier and the French flag being among the best known.

For Barthes this image is a mythical level symbol of French nationality and pride, of inclusiveness and **liberalism**, conveyed in the simplest of signs, and it is this level of analysis which **semiotics** claimed as its own. Semiotics has proved a very fruitful method of analysing advertising and cultural systems as a whole.

Technological determinism

A simple theory of social change which holds that any major change in society is the product of a change in tools and techniques.

The idea that technology, or productive techniques, drives social change is a widespread notion which has received much emphasis in the recent era of computer technology. In its most basic form it is an idea that claims that, for example, the steam engine caused the industrial revolution or that the invention of the computer has transformed all human relations (and some non-human). This kind of approach is often criticised, quite rightly, for being rather simplistic about the way in which technology operates within society. Economic, cultural and political factors often play an important role in the way that particular technologies are developed and used in society, and to trace the changes back just to the technology is reductionist.

The present era of excitement about what computer technology does, and can do, is a clear example of how mythologies about technology can be built up. At the one extreme we have endless claims of artificial intelligence, global cybernetic minds and living cyborgs, and at the other, billions of dollars were spent worldwide just before the turn of the last century to prevent computers from crashing because they could not recognise two particular digits. Admittedly that failure was built into their programs by humans who did not think ahead, which simply makes the point about the interaction of humans and technology. Karl Marx was sometimes a technological determinist, as are many commentators on computing, and as was Marshall McLuhan, the media theorist. Some commentators argue that, for some, technology is a new form of mysticism which allows the projection of fantasies onto neutral forms of control, reflecting a **technological determinism** that renders the world safe and controllable. Some of the discussions of **virtual reality** and the Internet clearly verge on the religious, or the reification and deification of abstract forces.

Terrorism

Acts of urban guerrillas or 'freedom fighters'. Also a type of writing.

The use of the term 'terrorist' to describe a political activist dedicated to the overthrow of a government or regime by force derives from the nineteenth century, in particular from the Russian terrorists who talked about the 'propaganda of the deed'. There are arguments that terrorism grew with the development of new technologies and mass communication, and is in part a product of the **anomie** produced by modern societies. The debate about the function and role of terrorism in modern politics is complicated by the role of the **mass media**, for whom terrorism, like crime, is an attractive story. The historical high point of urban terrorism was probably in the 1970s in Europe, and has declined somewhat since. The political focus has shifted back to the Middle East, and to a new form of religious fundamentalist terrorism which is aimed at the secular state, and at Israel and the West. There is also right-wing and state-sponsored terrorism, however, which plays an equally sinister role in world politics, particularly in Latin America. Terrorism at this level becomes a difficult process of naming, since it is also a political discourse which is involved with propaganda and control of the signifying process.

In the last decade the term has also been appropriated by postmodern theorists who use it to describe, not unsurprisingly, a mode of writing. This kind of **travelling theory** is character-istic of **postmodernism**, but one wonders about the usefulness of transposing a term which is closely associated with violence and death to describe a style of writing. Jean François Lyotard uses the term to suggest a typically male, aggressive way of writing which seeks to eliminate the opponent by exclusion from their shared language game. Gérard Gennette uses the term to connote a type of writing that refuses the literary, the poetic, or any accepted form of literary convention. It is a kind of 'in your face' postmodernism.

Thatcherism

A New Right ideology that represented an Anglo-American assault on social democracy.

The terms 'Thatcherism' and 'Reaganism' are sometimes used interchangeably, and there is a basic similarity in the outlook of both, which derives from their New Right ideas and their reli-ance on monetarism as a doctrine. It was Margaret Thatcher, elected head of state in Britain in 1979, who drew together the anti-union, pro-market and anti-inflationary ideas of different strands of the New Right, and gave them a populist coherence which swept her to power in three elections. Her impetus was an attack on the social–democratic consensus that had existed in Britain since the 1950s, and which had relied on ideas of full employment, government intervention and the welfare state.

Her ideas, which are also described as **economic rationalism**, revolved around the notion that the free operation of capitalist markets was the only way to develop economically, and that such market policies could only be implemented if the **state** was to refrain from intervention in the marketplace. These ideas led her to proclaim that the 'state should be rolled back' and private industries allowed to flourish in all areas, including areas formerly controlled by the state, such as transport, education, health and even prisons and welfare.

This economic rationalist ideology was embraced on both sides of the Atlantic, and Ronald Reagan in the US added a further anti-communist agenda to the idea of limiting the role of the state in the economy. Economic rationalist ideas of the limited role of the state led to the privatisation of previously nationalised industries, such as coal, gas, electricity, water and rail, and these policies were taken up in many countries in the advanced capitalist world. Since Thatcher's political demise in 1992 these ideas have come under attack, although they have also proved very resilient in many countries, but there has been increasing evidence of the long-term effects of such policies, one of which has been to widen economic inequalities. The credo that 'markets must decide' is Thatcher's political epithet and it remains a powerful **ideology**.

Travelling theory

A term describing the migration of theory in a global society.

This is a recent term, coined by the Palestinian–American writer and critic Edward Said, which describes the process whereby theory moves from place to place and from person to person. In a historical sense there is an implicit contrast with nineteenth-century imperial theory, which was nationalistic, Eurocentric and static in its conceptions of the world. The global interaction of cultures and media means that theory now travels far more quickly and profoundly, and there is a receptivity to theory which is itself a phenomenon of the post-60s era.

Said's use of the term also alluded to the way that there is something mobile in theory itself, a liberatory power that is enhanced as theory travels. The term **nomadic theory** is also used to describe this postmodern condition, and the relevance of the term is simply to reinforce the sense in which theory is no longer a local or national category but an intellectual resource that travels across cultures. At the same time there is a discussion of travel itself—of how experience of the rest of the world has changed the relationships of researcher and **culture**, of notions of the **other**—which has bred an understanding of location and space as relative. Perhaps travelling theory is simply a reflection of the **globalisation** of thought and of the inter-action of cultures and thought that it produces, but it is centrally a concern about change and transfusion, a metaphor of transition that deconstructs national boundaries.

Unconscious

The central term in psychoanalysis, it refers to that which is repressed from consciousness.

The discovery of the unconscious is central to Sigmund Freud's role as the father of **psychoanalysis**, although there is clear evidence that thinkers before Freud had used the term. Freud's clarification of the notion of the 'unconscious', and thereby of the importance of repression in the human psyche, is a key intellectual turning point in conceptions of the human. For many centuries the human subject had been thought of as a coherent, rational self and the discovery of the unconscious decentred this idea and demonstrated how the subject was a contradictory combination of the rational and the irrational. Freud argued that the human psyche was made up of distinct domains—the unconscious, the pre-conscious and the conscious—and that the repression of early memories and fears of castration and seduction, as well as instinctual desires, was the basis of unconscious life. Freud famously analysed these processes through looking at the way in which dreams worked and, in everyday speech, slips, symptoms and obsessions.

For Freud the unconscious is the site of repressed forces struggling to break into consciousness but held in check by a repressing **agency**. The repressing of instinctual drives, the most basic of which are hunger and sexuality, is what creates the dynamic process of consciousness, and the unconscious. The power of the unconscious in shaping the conscious life of the individual is very great, as demonstrated by the behaviour of obsessives, neurotics and pathologically disturbed individuals, and it is the power of the unconscious at the social level that makes Freud's work so important for **cultural studies**. In *Civilization and its Discontents*, Freud discussed the way in which repression necessarily operated in the reproduction of **society**, and thus began a major debate about how society controls its citizens through both conscious and unconscious means. Members of the **Frankfurt School** were among the first to seriously develop cultural analysis drawing on psychoanalysis, although Freud's ideas on the unconscious also permeated sociology and psychology.

Freud's analysis of the power of the unconscious developed into a full-blown social theory which attempted to explain both the origins of society, the role and basis of masculinity and femininity, and the function of the family in society. Without a theory of the unconscious, none of the rest would make sense, so we can say that repression is the real basis of Freud's social analysis. Many theorists have rejected Freud but his work has been highly influential across the humanities, and particularly in the way in which Jacques Lacan reworked Freud's theory of the unconscious through a linguistic **paradigm**. Lacan argued that the 'unconscious is structured like a language', by which he appears to mean that before the child acquires language through entry into the symbolic realm of **culture**, there is no repression and therefore no unconscious. The role of the unconscious in Lacanian theory is still central and, through his work on language, the idea of unconscious fantasy becomes very important in media and cultural studies.

Utilitarianism

A philosophical approach to ethics, based on common sense and empiricism, which advocates a practical analysis of the usefulness of things.

This was a very **Enlightenment** philosophy which applied reason to analysing human behaviour in the eighteenth and nineteenth centuries, and thereby further promoted the idea of rational man as the centre of the universe. Utilitarianism argued that actions were right in as much as they tended to promote happiness, wrong if they tended to produce the reverse of happiness. Put another way, this is to say that only pleasure is in itself good, and pain is evil in itself. This then allows a fairly clear analysis of the consequences of different kinds of actions, but it always assumes that the consequences of actions can be easily understood, which is far more debatable. Its historical rejection of traditional morality was progressive in its advocacy of reason rather than custom, but the complex problems of defining pain and pleasure, good and evil, have left utilitarianism in the Victorian era.

Utopia/Utopian

A term which refers to imagined societies or places where perfection and harmony exist.

Thomas More's *Utopia* (1516) began a long tradition of writing about imaginary and perfect societies and how they would function, although before him Plato had written in a similar vein in his *Republic*. This tradition has developed into science fiction, in which many forms of futuristic social organisation have been considered, both utopian and its opposite, dystopian. Many political movements demonstrate utopian tendencies, as do religious cults and mainstream organised religions. The term literally means 'no-place and somewhere ideal', which neatly summarises much of the literature in the area. Utopianism has always been a powerful force in art and literature, and is perhaps a necessary force in human thinking. However, utopian elements in politics and in cults have often had fairly disastrous consequences. Marxism has always had a strong utopian strain, an ideological approach which masqueraded as 'scientific socialism' and which was used to justify rather unattractive social policies. Art may necessarily sometimes be utopian, but a sense of **realism** in politics is probably preferable.

Virtual reality

A 3-D simulated world, which can either be a facsimile of the real thing, or an imaginary construct.

This is a term which began life as a description of a particular computer technology designed to produce a simulation of an actual environment, often for design or planning purposes, but which went on to designate a totally new reality which had little connection to the real. With recent developments in computer-generated imagery and interaction, individuals are said to inhabit virtual reality through a 'rig' consisting of a helmet with internal screens and a data-glove that allows manipulation of the environment. This produces a virtual reality which, it is claimed, is an out-of-body experience that transcends the ordinary and reaches another dimension. Much the same argument is effectively made in Jean Baudrillard's notion of 'hyperspace' or **hyperreality**, which is the image-based other dimension occupied by the **subject** in **postmodernism**.

The technological optimists view virtual reality as the greatest transformation of human experience since the invention of the wheel, and as unlocking the possibility of all kinds of new experience, but there is another viewpoint that sees it as merely wrap-around television. Virtual reality is always associated in some way with unrestricted pleasure, and perhaps this indicates its association with the way that dreams and fantasies play such an important part in electronic consumer culture.

Whiteness

A very recent term that makes clear that white people have, until now, seen themselves as the control subjects in any discussion of difference.

Nothing could demonstrate more clearly the Eurocentric assumptions of most western thought than the fact that most white thinkers haven't even noticed that they are a race; they simply take themselves as the natural **paradigm** against which everything else is, by default, measured. 'Whiteness' is a social construction so deeply imbued with its own naturalness, its taken-for-granted self-assurance, that even many left-wing theorists failed to notice its appearance. It is slightly ironic that Roland Barthes analysed the meaning of a photograph of a black French soldier in his *Mythologies* but could only see it in terms of its signification of 'Frenchness'; whiteness is the invisible **other** of colour. Only in the last decade has the idea of 'whiteness' appeared on the intellectual horizon and probably Toni Morrison's 1992 book *Playing in the Dark* put it there. From Aryan ideologies of racial supremacy to implicit notions of **civilisation** and **culture**, the theme of whiteness is a powerful **discourse** that is perhaps being considered for the first time as it begins to fissure. The realities of **multiculturalism** are beginning to expose the implicit assumptions of these constructions of whiteness, and the **deconstruction** of mythologies of historically specific social formations will prove interesting.

Writerly/Readerly

A distinction about the nature of texts made by Roland Barthes in his *S/Z* (1975).

Roland Barthes argues that some texts are of the 'lisable', or 'readerly', kind and others are of the 'scriptable', or 'writerly', sort. Texts of a writerly nature tend to be open, self-conscious almost, and make the reader work at confronting the complexity of language by resisting closure. Readerly texts, on the other hand, tend to be more conformist, to employ traditional realist techniques and to make life easy for the reader by assigning them a predetermined place. Writerly texts confront dominant forms while readerly texts tend to support them, a basic distinction which Barthes himself later complicates.

Bibliography

Abercrombie, N., Hill, S. and Turner, B. (eds) (1988) 'Max Weber' in *The Penguin Dictionary of Philosophy*, second edn, Harmondsworth: Penguin

Althusser, L. (1970) 'Ideology and ideological state apparatuses' in *Lenin and Philosophy and Other Essays* (trans. B. Brewster), London: New Left Books

Appadurai, Arjun (ed.) (1986) *The Social Life of Things: Commodities in Cultural Perspective*, Cambridge: Cambridge University Press

Aristotle, *The Politics* (trans. T.A. Sinclair), Harmondsworth: Penguin

Bakhtin, Mikhail (1984) *Rabelais and His World* (trans. H. Iwolsky), Indiana: Indiana University Press

Barrett, Michele (1991) *The Politics of Truth: From Marx to Foucault*, Cambridge: Polity Press

Barthes, Roland (1957) *Mythologies* (trans. A. Lavers), London: Granada

—— (1965/1977) *Elements of Semiology* (trans. A. Lavers and C. Smith), New York: Farrar, Straus & Giroux

—— (1975) *S/Z* (trans. R. Millar), Oxford: Blackwell

—— (1977) 'The death of the author' (trans. S. Heath), in S. Heath (ed.) *Images, Music, Text*, London: Collins

Berger, John (1972) *Ways of Seeing*, London: BBC/Harmondsworth: Penguin

Bhaba, Homi (1994) *The Location of Culture*, London: Routledge

Bloom, Harold (1995) *The Western Canon*, London: Papermac

Bourdieu, Pierre (1973) *The Field of Cultural Production*, New York: Columbia University Press

—— (1990) *The Logic of Practice*, Cambridge: Polity Press

Butler, Judith (1993) *Bodies that Matter: On the Discursive Limits of Sex*, London: Routledge

Cohen, Stanley (1987) *Folk Devils and Moral Panics*, revised edn, Oxford: Blackwell

Creed, Barbara (1993) *The Monstrous Feminine*, London: Routledge

de Beauvoir, Simone (1972) *The Second Sex*, Harmondsworth: Penguin

Debord, Guy (1970 [1967]) *Society of the Spectacle*, Detroit: Black & Red

Deleuze, Gilles (1985) 'Nomad thought' in D.B. Allison (ed.) *The New Nietzsche*, Cambridge, Mass.: MIT Press

Derrida, Jacques (1967) *Of Grammatology*, Baltimore, MD: Johns Hopkins University Press

Durkheim, Emile (1951 [1897]) *Suicide*, Glencoe: Free Press

Dyer, Richard (1986) *Heavenly Bodies*, Basingstoke: Macmillan

Fanon, Franz (1986 [1952]) *Black Skins, White Masks*, London: Pluto Press

—— (1952) 'The fact of blackness' in *Black Skins, White Masks*

Foucault, Michel (1971) 'The order of discourse' in R. Young (ed.) *Untying the Text*, London: Routledge

—— (1972) *The Archaeology of Knowledge* (trans. A.M. Sheridan Smith), London: Tavistock

—— (1973) *The Order of Things*, New York: Vintage Books

—— (1979) *The History of Sexuality*, vol. 1, London: Allen Lane

—— (1986a) 'What is an author?' (trans. J.V. Harari) in P. Rainbow (ed.) *The Foucault Reader*, Harmondsworth: Penguin

—— (1986b) 'Of other spaces', *Diacritics*, Spring, pp. 22–7

Freud, Sigmund (1930) *Civilization and its Discontents*, Standard Edition 4, London: Hogarth

Gilroy, P. (1993) *The Black Atlantic: Modernity and Double Consciousness*, London: Verso

Hall, Stuart (1989) 'The meaning of New Times' in S. Hall and M. Jacques (eds) *New Times*, London: Lawrence & Wishart

—— (1996a) 'New ethnicities' in D. Morley and K.H. Chen (eds) *Stuart Hall: Critical Dialogues in Cultural Studies*, London: Routledge

—— (1996b) 'The question of cultural identity' in S. Hall et al. (eds) *Modernity*, London: Blackwell

Hall, Stuart et al. (1978) *Policing the Crisis: Mugging, the State and Law and Order*, London: Macmillan

Haraway, Donna (1985) 'A manifesto for cyborgs: science, technology and socialist feminism in the 1980s', in L. Nicholson (ed.) (1990) *Feminism/Postmodernism*, London: Routledge

Hoggart, Richard (1998) *The Uses of Literacy*, Harmondsworth: Penguin

hooks, bell (1994) *Outlaw Culture: Resisting Representation*, London: Routledge

Jameson, Fredric (1984) 'Postmodernism, or the cultural logic of late capitalism', *New Left Review*, no. 146

—— (1991) *Postmodernism or the Cultural Logic of Late Capitalism*, Durham, NC: Duke University Press

Kristeva, Julia (1974) *Revolution in Poetic Language* (trans. L.S. Roudiez), New York: Columbia University Press

—— (1982) *Powers of Horror: An Essay on Abjection* (trans. L.S. Roudiez), New York: Columbia University Press

Leavis, F.R. (1930) *Man, Civilisation and Minority Culture*, London: Minority Press

Leavis, Q.D. (1968) *Fiction and the Reading Public*, London: Chatto & Windus

Lévi-Strauss, Claude (1976) *The Savage Mind*, Chicago: Chicago University Press

Lyotard, Jean-François (1984) *The Postmodern Condition: A Report on Knowledge*, Manchester: Manchester University Press

McLuhan, Marshall and Fiore, Quentin (1967) *The Medium is the Message*, London: Allen Lane

More, Thomas (1951 [1516]), *Utopia*, (trans. R. Robinson), London: Penguin Classics

Morrison, Toni (1992) *Playing in the Dark*, Cambridge, MA: Harvard University Press

Mulvey, Laura (1975) 'Visual pleasure and narrative cinema' in L. Mulvey, *Visual and Other Pleasures*, London: Macmillan

Norris, Christopher (1982) *Deconstruction: Theory and Practice*, London: Routledge

Plato, (1976) *The Republic*, (trans. A. D. Lindsay), London: Dent

Said, Edward (1978) *Orientalism*, London: Routledge

Sarap, Madan (1996) *Identity, Culture and the Postmodern World*, Edinburgh: Edinburgh University Press

Schlesinger, Arthur, (1999) *The Disuniting of America*, New York: W.W. Norton

Weber, Max to come

Williams, Raymond (1961) *Culture and Society*, Harmondsworth: Penguin

—— (1981) *Culture*, London: Fontana

Wilson, Edward (1975) *Sociobiology: The New Synthesis*, Cambridge, MA: Belknap Press/Harvard University Press